ask the
BIBLE
GEEK

fascinating

answers

to intriguing

questions

mark hart

servant

AN IMPRINT OF
FRANCISCAN MEDIA
Cincinnati, Ohio

Cover design by Kathleen Lynch | Black Kat Design
Book design by Mark Sullivan

LIBRARY OF CONGRESS CONTROL NUMBER: 2015932430

ISBN 978-1-61636-896-8

Published by Servant Books, an imprint of Franciscan Media
28 W. Liberty St.
Cincinnati, OH 45202
www.FranciscanMedia.org

Printed in the United States of America.
Printed on acid-free paper
17 18 19   5 4

To my children, Hope, Trinity, Faith, and Josiah—may the Word of God dwell in you richly, and may you learn as much about the Father's love from his Word as I have learned from all of you.

Contents

Dealing with Life's Temptations and Trials

The high road to heaven has its potholes ... 59

Walking the Walk

Catholic Christianity is not for wimps ... 93

Finding God in the Everyday

He's everywhere...just take a look ... 131

Acknowledgments

There are far too many people in my life to thank for their love and support.

I've been blessed with family and friends, mentors and colleagues, priests and religious, who have all offered me invaluable insights into the heart of God through their living, daily witness.

No soul, however, has taught me more about the tender love and gentle compassion of God as my wife, Melanie, continues to do. Without her love and her constant sacrifices, nothing I attempt to do "in the Name of the Lord" would come to fruition. Every word I speak or write is made possible only by God's mercy, my family's sacrifices, and their united belief that the love of God must be shared.

So, thank you to my family for who they are and all they do.

And most importantly, praise and thanksgiving to my heavenly Father, who looks through my constant unworthiness and somehow finds worth. You are the air I breathe. I stand in awe of your dangerous and sacramental wonders. You chose the nails, and it has been through the scars in my life that I have found peace, hope, and healing. When I feared that you had abandoned me, you drew closest, and for that, I am yours for the taking. I pray you give me "work until my life is over, and life until my work is done." I love you, Abba.

Being mindless is easy. How often do you get into your car and forget where you are going, or in the middle of a conversation stop and ask, "What was I saying?" It's easier to watch television than to read a book. It's easier to hit the drive-through than stop and make dinner. It's easier on a first date to see a movie than to go for a walk. Why? Because the second options each require thought and necessitate attention.

Look around yourself right now. Do you see God? He is there. It's unfortunate that we cannot more easily see God in our midst on a daily basis. Stress has become the norm, time is something "we just don't have," and nobody seems to understand our unique position on anything. And in the midst of life's never-ending busyness, we run through our walk with Christ. I have always believed that the greatest gift we can give one another as human beings is to invite the next person to think.

God is right beside you right now, in both obvious and not-so-obvious ways. The question needs to change from "Who is God?" or "Where is God?" to "How is God?" How is God working in my life today? How is God making his presence known to me? How is God answering my prayers (and he is)? How do I approach God? How do I look for God? How do I trust God with my life?

The first thing I have to do is realize that God is God and I am not. The second thing I have to do is put God's will before my own. The third thing I have to do is trust that God has a plan for me. And the fourth thing I have to do is be open to his call.

The wisest thing I learned during my years in college I heard not in a classroom but over a basket of buffalo wings. A good friend looked at me and said, "Fish swim. Birds fly." Pretty profound, huh? What he meant was that we give glory to God by doing what we are designed to do.

I am realistic, and I know where my talents do and do not rest. I cannot sing in an opera, I cannot solve difficult mathematical equations, and I cannot hit a hundred-mile-per-hour fastball. I can give glory to God in other ways, though, by utilizing what he has given me to work with.

I am not a scholar; I am just a geek...a Bible geek. This book is not intended to explain all the foundational and universal truths of Christianity. It's not meant to be an in-depth explanation of Scripture in our world today. It's a lot simpler than that.

I love to read the Bible. I have a weird sense of humor. I find no greater challenge or joy than to encounter the extraordinary (God) in the ordinary (the world) on a daily basis. The timelessness of God's truth is contained within this work, not in the words that I have written but in the Word that God himself inspired so many centuries ago.

I have often said that I could care less whether or not anyone ever read a single word of mine, as long as they read every single word of his. God's Word is power, truth, and joy. God's Word exposes, challenges, convicts, and transforms, cutting through generations in time like a scalpel cuts between flesh and bone (Hebrews 4:12).

That's what Christ does, and that is what the Incarnation is all about: enculturation. God came right into human culture—born into the dirt, the hopelessness, and the sin of the world. Christ transforms whores into saints and murderers into martyrs. That same Christ can transform our biblical ignorance or illiteracy into wisdom and luminance if we let him.

If you're looking for the key that will unlock the biblical and theological universe, put this book down. I think you'll need a book that is far weightier (and, uh, more boring). The stories and analogies in this book are not designed to be earth-shatteringly theological, nor am I setting out to answer the greatest questions about Scripture. As I see it, I'm basically here to do two things: to love God and laugh often. I'm not making anything more out of this book, so neither should you.

On the other hand, if you, like me, are just a sinner on a journey, struggling to make sense out of this world around you, hoping to find some joy or peace or truth, well then, read on.

And to any future biblical scholars who may be reading this right now, this goes doubly for you. It's not enough to know the words; we need to know the author. Never forget that the Word of God exists to be lived, not just studied. Every once in a while, close the books and go play with a dog, hold a baby, or take in a sunset. Rediscover the life-altering joy that comes from simply living in his presence.

I hope that you enjoy this compilation of Bible Geek messages, but I pray that you will put this book down frequently. We can never allow ourselves as children of our heavenly Father to spend more time reading books about Jesus than reading Jesus himself, uniquely present in his inspired Word. While reading thoughts about God in a book can help us envision the Lord in new ways, nothing can replace the grace we receive by reading about God in his Book.

Much like an appetizer, reflections on God's Word are intended merely to whet the appetite. The main course of Scripture and Eucharist are waiting to nourish and fulfill us, to bring life, and to uplift our souls, continually leading us back to his mercy and to his table, the altar where we are forever altered.

The Word of God draws you and me more fully into the sacramental Church, the apostolic tradition, and the incarnational Christ, found most specifically and undeniably in the Holy Eucharist. Dive into the

Bible, and allow the Lord to radically transform your life.

Are you a Bible geek?

"Jesus said…'I am'" (John 8:58).

—Mark Hart, Bible Geek

GETTING
TO KNOW
THE
TRINITY

It's
the ultimate
three-for-one
deal

What's in a name?

> God has highly exalted him and bestowed on him the name
> which is above every name, that at the name of Jesus every knee
> should bow.
> —PHILIPPIANS 2:9–10

Have you ever been called a nickname that was less than flattering? Has anyone ever made fun of your family name or of your parents? How did it make you feel? Why is taking the Lord's name in vain such a big deal? Why is it listed up there with "Thou shalt not kill"? Well, there's a lot to a name in God's eyes.

Solution Offered

Have you ever been in a store and seen one of those spinning racks or displays holding little cards with peoples' names across the top? Each name has a different meaning, like "gentle one," "strong warrior," or "holy friend." In the eyes of God, names aren't just "labels" to tell people apart. Your name is connected to your "essence"; it speaks of who you are.

In the Old Testament God changed Abram to Abraham, Jacob to Israel, Sarai to Sara. In the New Testament, Jesus changed Simon's name to Peter, because through God's grace Simon's essence (everything about him) was changed by God.

God's name is important, too. It, too, expresses his essence. A few thousand years ago, you couldn't even say God's name; you'd be stoned to death. Nowadays, some people can't even make it through a sentence without using the name of the Lord as a swear word.

Some people say, "If God's so big, why would he care what I call him? He's God; he's got other things to worry about."

The answer: God is that big. The Creator of all creation is totally perfect and totally holy. Taking his name in vain doesn't make God any less holy, but it does make his name less holy in the eyes of the world.

When we who call ourselves Catholic Christians violate this commandment (or allow others to constantly disrespect God by destroying his holy name in front of us), we are not living up to our call as children of God. Why are so many people willing to fight to defend the honor and name of their mom or dad or family but unwilling to stand up for our Father who is in heaven?

Notice that St. Paul tells us that at the name of Jesus, every knee must bow. This may not happen on a daily basis down here on earth, but the Bible tells us that one day it will. Let's make it our goal to change the way others speak about our Father. It seems like the very least we can do for our God who has given us so much and done so much for us—and who loves us, forgives us, and will never leave us.

Salvation Given

God has highly exalted him and bestowed on him the name which is above every name, that at the name of Jesus every knee should bow.
—PHILIPPIANS 2:9–10

4

Pray then like this:
Our Father who art in heaven,
hallowed be thy name.
—MATTHEW 6:9

What is your relationship with God like? Who is he to you? Is he a supreme but cold, faraway being who controls our lives like a puppet master? Is he sort of a judge who sits on high sending people to hell? Is he a strict disciplinarian who doesn't want us to have any fun?

Solution Offered

Well, the answer is right here in this verse from Matthew. God is our Father, a dad who wants the best for his children. He loves us enough to forgive us, direct us, and offer us words of wisdom and guidelines to live by (the Commandments), as well as an example (Jesus) and a conscience (the Holy Spirit).

St. Teresa used to say that this verse was so incredible that she often would meditate on it for hours, unable to complete the Lord's Prayer (the Our Father), which follows in the Matthew passage. She had a difficult time comprehending that God, the all-knowing Creator of all, wanted us to love him and know him as a daddy.

Some people have a pretty easy time relating to Jesus, or the Holy Spirit, but then have an incredibly difficult time relating to God. Why is that? God is our Father, it says right there in the passage. (Way to go, St. Matthew.)

Some people think that it's because God is our Father and because so many people have somewhat cold or impersonal relationships with their own fathers. This is not to say that people don't have great, respectful, loving friendships with their dads. Rather, it is to say that most people tend to associate their moms with caring, affectionate, outward displays of love and their fathers with hard, disciplined, less affectionate examples of parenthood.

That same feeling was alive and kickin' in Jesus's day. Most men during Jesus's day didn't show affection, which is one of the reasons that Jesus shocked so many people on a daily basis. Jesus was so outwardly loving, caring, forgiving, and affirming that people couldn't believe a man would be that way in public, especially to strangers, lepers, and sinners!

Jesus wants you to encounter God and go to God as his child, as a little boy or little girl, dying to be picked up and held in his arms. Do it now, today. Say three Our Fathers. And don't just rattle them off as if you're going for the world prayer-sprint record. Take your time. Spend a good few seconds on each and every word. Think about what you're saying.

At the end of the Our Fathers, ask God for greater trust in him, like a child should have in a parent, and for the courage and the humble discipline it takes to follow him completely. He won't let you down.

Salvation Given

Pray then like this:
Our Father who art in heaven,
hallowed be thy name.
—Matthew 6:9

Dad is spelled the same way backwards and forwards, maybe it's because the Father loves us the same no matter if we are running toward him or running away from his love. Here's a hint: Run to him.

For I, the Lord your God,
> hold your right hand;
it is I who say to you, "Fear not,
> I will help you."
—ISAIAH 41:13

As a child, were you in a hurry to grow up? Did your parents ever embarrass you? Have you ever asked your parents for more freedom, privacy, or responsibility?

Solution Offered

I was sitting at a stoplight the other day and saw a father and his young son (probably about four years old) waiting to cross the street. When the signal changed, the child raised an open hand to his father. The dad then took him by the hand, and they carefully made their way to the other side of the street.

As I watched them, I was reminded of this passage. Here God is saying to Isaiah, "Stick with me, kid. Give me your hand, and I'll lead you through this sometimes dangerous and difficult world."

Why was Isaiah successful? Isaiah allowed himself to be led by the Lord, instead of trying to do everything on his own (like most of us try to do).

When I was a kid, I always reached for my mom's or dad's hand before crossing the street. The world was much bigger then. As I grew up, though, I quit reaching for it. In fact, it got to a point in junior high and high school where I was embarrassed of my parents because of the things that they'd say, or the car they drove, or whatever. I would even make Mom drop me off a block or two away from the mall, just so I wouldn't be seen getting out of her minivan (with the wood paneling on the sides).

I feel foolish about that now, especially given how much my parents love me and how many sacrifices they made to put food on our table and clothes on our backs.

It's the same with God, I think. Around junior high and high school, many of us might feel a little awkward about being "seen" with God or even opening our hand(s) to him, even at church. We forget how much he loves us and the sacrifice he made for us, the greatest sacrifice: being nailed to a cross so many years ago.

Remember what Jesus tells us in Matthew 10:33, "Whoever denies me before others, I will deny before my heavenly Father" (NRSV).

We should never be ashamed of our parent(s)—including our heavenly Parent. This week, let's really allow ourselves to be led by God. Let's open our palms when we pray and allow our Father in heaven to take us by the hand and lead us through the dangerous intersections of life.

Salvation Given

For I, the Lord your God,
   hold your right hand;
it is I who say to you, "Fear not,
   I will help you."
—ISAIAH 41:13

Be sure to look both ways before crossing the street; but also remember that God's got you in the palm of his hand (see Isaiah 49:16).

Truly, I say to you, whoever does not receive the kingdom of God like a child shall not enter it.

—MARK 10:15

Do you ever feel old? Do you sometimes wish you could go be a kid again, without worries or stress or expectations? Without responsibilities? Things sure were simple as a kid. Jesus says that things can still be that simple.

Solution Offered

Let me ask you, "Are you a child of God or a brat of God?"

A child takes what the parent gives. A brat whines when the item given isn't exactly what he or she wants.

A child depends on the parent for everything. A brat goes to the parent only when in need.

A child has manners and says "please" and "thank you." A brat has orders and says "now!" or, "you just don't love me."

A child does what the parent says. A brat does what he or she wants.

A child runs to the parents and wants to be with them. A brat waits until called.

A child is open to help and advice. A brat refuses to accept help or ask for it.

A child admits being wrong or bad. A brat blames everybody else when in trouble.

Now, these are generalizations, but you get my point.

God tells us that we need to be like children because kids are joyfully obedient and humbly dependent. I think I'm more like a brat most of the time, to be honest. Instead of trusting God and submitting to his will and his Commandments, usually I would rather spend my time looking for loopholes, trying to find ways to cut corners or justify the sins that I commit. Does this sound familiar to any of you?

Start today and try to become more childlike. Have fun, don't be afraid to act like a dork, and laugh at yourself. The only reason to take this life too seriously is if it's your only one. Live for heaven! Make it your goal to view life and the world with the same newness and awe that you did when you were tiny.

Praise and thank God for all of the important people in your life, even if some of them drive you crazy. Honor God by being obedient to your parents and more patient with your brothers and sisters. When you look at your family, thank God for them.

God has set aside his kingdom for the childlike—for those who are loving enough to trust and obey him and humble enough to depend on him.

Salvation Given

> Truly, I say to you, whoever does not receive the kingdom of God like a child shall not enter it.
> —Mark 10:15

Growing old is mandatory; growing up is optional.

For with God nothing will be impossible.

—LUKE 1:37

"He'll never change." "That'll never happen." "We'll never agree."
Never may be a word we use, but I was reading through God's
dictionary the other day (he invited me to his house for a barbecue.
Adam was making his famous ribs, Eve made applesauce, and Moses
was making "manna-cotti"), and the word *never* isn't in God's dictionary.
Why?

This might be the easiest verse to memorize out of any that we've
looked at so far. Memorize this one. Learn it. Know the chapter and
verse. This is one that we should never—oops, I mean it is a verse we
must remember.

I'm often amazed at how little faith I have. There have been situations in my life when I'd say things like you read above—like, "No
matter what happens, they'll never change." Sometime later God
always seems to knock me off my seat and remind me that I can't ever
say that someone will never change, because I don't know the will of
God, and I can't begin to understand how deep his love and mercy are.

St. Augustine is now known as one of the greatest thinkers and saints
of our Church, but he didn't surrender his life to God until well into the
middle of his life—and only after years upon years of intense, consistent, and sincere prayer by his mother, Monica (also a saint—well, she
had better be after all that prayer, huh?).

The mere fact that we humans use the word *never* so often just goes
to show how little faith we have. But remember what the Holy Spirit is

saying through St. Luke's pen today: "With God nothing will be impossible." That area of your life that you struggle with, don't surrender to it. Keep fighting it, keep trying, keep offering it up in prayer, and someday, with God's help, you will win out.

That person in your life whom you want to give up on—the one who constantly hurts you or themselves, the one who won't listen to you no matter how hard you try—that's the one you need to keep praying for, because through prayer, the will of God will be done in that relationship. This doesn't mean that we should stay in an unhealthy relationship or allow people to continue to hurt us; it means that we need to be big enough people to pray for those who hurt us or make our lives more difficult (Matthew 5:44).

Just remember to never, never, never, never, never, never, never, never, never, never, never say never when you're talking about God or dealing with God, because what does Luke tell us in chapter 1, verse 37, everybody?

You got it! I've never been prouder. Um, what I, uh, what I mean is that I can't think of a time in which I have been prouder of you.

Salvation Given

For with God nothing will be impossible.
—LUKE 1:37

Never underestimate the power to change yourself. (Oops, there I go again.)

They stripped him...plaiting a crown of thorns they put it on his head.... And kneeling before him they mocked him.... They spat upon him...and struck him on the head.... And [they] led him away to crucify him.

—Matthew 27:28–31

Ever heard the term *excruciating pain*? Do you know where it comes from? The word actually had to be invented. No one had a word to describe a pain as intense as a crucifixion, so a new word was created. The word *excruciating* literally means "out of the cross."

Solution Offered

In today's society, it's not always popular to tell the truth. Talking about what really happened on that hill two thousand years ago makes people uncomfortable. But Jesus didn't go through what he went through to have it sugarcoated.

What really happened? Read on, if you can take it. Good Friday isn't about what's comfortable. If you want to truly live as a Christian, however, you should get comfortable with being uncomfortable. You don't have to read this, but it couldn't hurt—not like it hurt him.

He was so overcome with stress and anxiety that he sweat blood. It's called hematidrosis. Chemicals break down the capillaries in the sweat glands, releasing blood. Ever been that stressed?

He was stripped in public. Can you imagine the humiliation?

He was whipped and beaten. Each whip, made of braided leather with metal balls and hooks woven into each strap, imbedded in and tore the flesh, up to thirty-nine times from each soldier.

Thorns were placed upon his head, piercing his scalp. Ever cut your head?

He was struck on the head by a heavy reed, several times.

His muscles and nerve endings exposed, every movement sent intense pain throughout his body as the heavy crossbeam was given him to bear.

His every movement, every jolt, agitated and reopened his wounds. He couldn't move an inch without feeling the pain. The narrow city streets offered no respite from the jostling of the crowd.

Suffering from intense dehydration, his kidneys stopped working, and his body could not produce fluids. His heart was racing to pump blood that wasn't there. His blood pressure dropped, making him collapse and faint. And there wasn't a doctor around.

He had nine-inch spikes driven through his wrists, piercing the Median nerves. Take the pain of hitting your "funny bone" and multiply it by a thousand.

His arms were stretched at least six inches, dislocating both of his shoulders. I've dislocated my shoulder—the worst pain I've ever experienced.

His feet were nailed to the crossbeam, pain shooting throughout his body.

Raised up by ropes, his flesh tore.

He went into respiratory acidosis—meaning carbon dioxide in the blood was dissolved as carbonic acid, increasing the acidity of the blood and leading to a very irregular, erratic heartbeat.

Fluid gathered around the heart in the membrane, a condition known as pericardial effusion. Around the lungs, pleural effusion caused by the sustained rapid heart rate slowly destroyed the entire internal system.

His intense blood loss caused him to go into hypovolemic shock, basically shutting his body down.

Unable to lift himself to breathe anymore, intensely dehydrated, muscles failing, blood pressure falling—he breathed his last, handing over his spirit, finishing Passover.

He had a lance thrust through his side, piercing his lung.

For Jesus, it wasn't about his own needs or will; it was about his Father's will and the needs of the many (you and me).

For you, right now in your life, this week, who is it about? Is it about your will, your needs—or his?

If you answered that it's about you, what would it take for you to change? What else would God himself, Jesus Christ, beyond the crucifixion, need to endure for us to put him first?

Salvation Given

They stripped him...plaiting a crown of thorns they put it on his head.... And kneeling before him they mocked him.... They spat upon him...and struck him on the head.... And [they] led him away to crucify him.

—MATTHEW 27:28–31

It's called the Passion because that's how he loves you—passionately.

He works for my salvation.

> But Jesus answered them, "My Father is still working, and I also
> am working." For this reason the Jews were seeking all the more
> to kill him, because he was not only breaking the sabbath, but was
> also calling God his own Father, thereby making himself equal
> to God.
> —JOHN 5:17–18

Why was Jesus a carpenter?

Solution Offered

There were a variety of popular and common occupations in Jesus's
time. Some men were farmers, some shepherds, some fishermen.
Others were teachers, traders, merchants, or servants; many were
slaves. St. Paul actually made a living as a tentmaker.

It is a well-known fact that Jesus's earthly father, Joseph, was a
carpenter. Carpentry was a noble and humble trade, respected yet not
adored or revered. What is interesting is that there is really only one
explicit Scripture passage in the Gospels that tells us that Jesus himself
worked as a carpenter. Even if the passage didn't tell us that, however,
it could be assumed that he did, since Joseph was one.

Back then, sons watched and learned the trade of their fathers. They
obeyed and served them, working alongside of them each day. As time
went on, the listening and watching turned into actual hands-on time,
assisting and then working side by side until eventually the son would
take over the trade from the father.

This process is exactly what Jesus would have gone through as he
matured into physical manhood. It is also what Jesus would have done
as he matured into divine manhood, following the example and will of

his heavenly Father. When the moment came for Jesus to reveal both his identity and mission, it was as though Clark Kent took off his glasses and publicly put on Superman's cape. Jesus had followed, listened to, and watched his heavenly Father at work, and eventually the time came to reveal his own vocation, to put his "trade" to work. Jesus perfectly imitates his heavenly Father and is completely obedient to him, as we read in John 5:19–24:

> Jesus said to them, "Truly, truly, I say to you, the Son can do nothing of his own accord, but only what he sees the Father doing; for whatever he does, that the Son does likewise. For the Father loves the Son, and shows him all that he himself is doing; and greater works than these will he show him, that you may marvel. For as the Father raises the dead and gives them life, so also the Son gives life to whom he will. The Father judges no one, but has given all judgment to the Son, that all may honor the Son, even as they honor the Father. He who does not honor the Son does not honor the Father who sent him. Truly, truly, I say to you, he who hears my word and believes him who sent me, has eternal life; he does not come into judgment, but has passed from death to life."

I have learned many things from my earthly father. He taught me (and all my siblings) a strong work ethic—how important it is to take pride in your work. He taught us the importance of respect, both of self and of others. He taught us the importance of family, integrity, and upholding the family name. He taught us to speak our mind with conviction and to admit when we were wrong. He taught us to look out for one another and for those who cannot or will not look out for themselves, whether family, friends, or strangers.

My earthly father taught us these things not simply because he is a good man, husband, and father, but because he believes in God and in what God teaches. I don't have to listen to my father, but I choose to do so. Additionally, while I may share my father's physical appearance, values, and genes, we share something even greater: blood.

In the end, as Christians, we have a choice whether or not to listen to our heavenly Father and live as he is calling us to do. Jesus gives us the perfect example to follow. We never have to wonder how we should act to make our Father proud—we need only to look at the Gospels and at the example of Christ.

We all may have different physical blood types on earth, but spiritually we all share the same blood: the blood of the Father, the blood that was shed for us and washed away our sins. That's why Jesus mounted the cross for us—it was the most undeniable blood test the world has ever known. The cross of Christ leaves no doubt who our true Father is, and who we are called to imitate and emulate.

The test results have come in: God is your father; he's your daddy. The negative blood test of Good Friday has been made positive through our big brother's resurrection and the waters of our baptism. Welcome to the family.

Salvation Given

But Jesus answered them, "My Father is still working, and I also am working." For this reason the Jews were seeking all the more to kill him, because he was not only breaking the sabbath, but was also calling God his own Father, thereby making himself equal to God.
—JOHN 5:17–18

My prayer is that, when people look at me, they can see the resemblance to my father.

Let's talk about love.

He died for all, that those who live might live no longer for themselves but for him.

—2 CORINTHIANS 5:15

Who is the most important person in your life? So, who is it? Who is the most important person in your life, right now, today?

Solution Offered

Many of us would respond with the name of a family member, or a boyfriend or girlfriend, or husband or wife. Some would respond with the name of their best friend.

Think hard; I'll wait. Of all of the people in your life today, whom do you care about the most? Who means the most to you? Whose happiness means the most to you?

The sad truth is that as much as we love or care about another person, there are many of us alive today who will find the answer to this question not in one another but in the mirror.

For years my favorite two phrases were "I don't want to" and "because I don't feel like it." I was a very selfish person. Actually, it hurts to say this, but I still am pretty selfish sometimes. As much as I care about others (or claim to), a lot of times, I still put my wants and needs ahead of others' because I feel like it, or it's more comfortable, or it's easier.

What if Jesus had done that instead of hanging on that cross?

Make no mistake: Nails didn't keep Jesus on that cross; love did.

That person you thought of first, or those people you thought of, when I asked you who is most important: Would they die for you? Truthfully? Would Jesus? Yes. Did Jesus? Yes. Does that really mean anything to you? Yes.

That's love, true love: to be willing to die for another (see John 15:13).

So this verse from 2 Corinthians is telling us two things:

Real love means sacrifice and death. If the person who says, "I love you," is not willing to sacrifice for you—it ain't love.

If we want to experience true love, we need to put our own needs and wants second to God's.

He has a plan for you. You can follow it, or you can fight it. Your choice. Just remember, the easy way out is just that—the easy way out. And anything easy has its cost.

Salvation Given

He died for all, that those who live might live no longer for themselves but for him.

—2 CORINTHIANS 5:15

This week, have more faith in God. He has faith in you.

It's closer than you might think.

They found the stone rolled away from the tomb, but when they
went in they did not find the body.
—LUKE 24:2–3

Does God dwell inside of you? Do you think God is within you?

.   *Solution Offered*

They laid Jesus in the tomb and rolled a stone in front of it. What was
the tomb like? What did it smell like? Think about the tomb…what an
amazing place it must have been! The tomb went from being this dark
place, a place of death, surrounded by stone, into being a place of life,
of rebirth—a place to start over. When opened, the tomb allowed the
sunlight in and the Son's light out.

That's how it is with our hearts. Our hearts, in way, are like the tomb
that held Christ. God breathes life into us, we are born and baptized,
and Christ dwells within our hearts. For many of us, however, who
either don't know Jesus, don't want to follow him yet, or are afraid to
trust in him completely, our hearts become the tomb of Holy Saturday
instead of the tomb of Easter Sunday.

As life changes, so do our priorities. Most of us go to high school
and college and then begin working, and slowly many of us become
blinded. We forget (or pretend to forget) what is most important. We
think more about ourselves than others, or we believe that we can't
have fun or really live and still be Christian. Being rich, being seen,
being in the right group, having the right car, and securing the right
job all begin to take priority over God and our relationship with him.
We become hardened by the world, and we don't even know it—

so hardened, in fact, that our hearts become like stone, not allowing the light in or out.

The world would rather keep Christ in that tomb, locked away in the darkness. If Christ stays in there, people can just continue doing what they want, without guilt, or pain, or fear of judgment. Our culture says that we don't need Christ...that the Easter story isn't real and didn't really happen. Modern minds will often tell you that all you need to do is think for yourself—and about yourself.

Hmm, "think about yourself"—that reminds me of a couple who ate some fruit in a garden once.

As Jesus's body was destroyed, so was our debt and our death. With his new life, you and I have a new chance, the chance for eternal life. What are you doing with that chance? Is your heart like the tomb of Holy Saturday? Are you hiding the light of Christ within you? Is your heart like stone? If so, what's holding you back?

Move the stone. Break down the walls. Invite Christ to truly take control of your life. I know it's scary, but it's not as scary as death, actual death. Remember, you and I are not beating death without Christ— and that's all there is to it.

Salvation Given

> They found the stone rolled away from the tomb, but when they went in they did not find the body.
> —LUKE 24:2–3

Open your tomb today, and if you need help moving the rock, ask God for it.

When he had said this, he breathed on them and said to them,
"Receive the Holy Spirit."
—JOHN 20:22

Do you ever find yourself out of breath?

Solution Offered

My friend and I walked up a very, very long flight of stairs today. I'm
talking really long. It was like walking to the top of the Empire State
Building (minus about sixty flights of stairs or so, but you get the idea).
When we were nearing the rooftop level, neither of us wanted to be the
first to admit how out of breath we were…we were being guys. Then
we both sort of laughed and admitted to one another that neither of us
had been running every day like we used to do.

My legs were weak and my heart was pounding. At one point, halfway
up, I may have prayed for a quick death. Three-quarters of the way to
our destination, I think I even heard my guardian angel begging me to
turn back.

When we finally stopped climbing, my muscles were burning, I was
sweating profusely, and my legs finally gave out as I fell to my knees,
gasping for breath.

It was then that it hit me: Breathing is really important. I know, what
a landmark statement. Seriously, though, how often do you stop and
consider how vital breathing is to life? It's usually not until we are out
of breath or straining for breath (like underwater) that we really stop to
consider just how important something so common is to our existence.
Then something else hit me. The Greek word for the Holy Spirit is
pneuma, which means "breath" or "wind."

Think about it. What an awesome reminder from God of his presence in our lives at every moment: breathing. Most of the time, breathing is an unconscious action that we don't even stop to notice. Most of the time, too, even in Christian's lives, the Holy Spirit is the same way— the Spirit is an active presence that we don't often stop to notice. When you hold your breath long enough, however, you either notice the need for air—or you are dead. Likewise, when we are not open to the Holy Spirit, sooner or later we will notice that there is something missing in our life, maybe even that we have become spiritually dead.

If you have ever had a really powerful experience of the Holy Spirit at Mass, or on a retreat, or during reconciliation, then you know the power of the Spirit I'm talking about. It is a power so real and so beautifully overwhelming that you will feel like you just climbed a mountain but still have the energy to keep climbing!

As usual, God is not only beautiful in his mystery but subtle in his irony, for when we truly experience the Spirit, this breath of life, we are often left almost breathless—and often speechless.

Right now, since many of you are consciously thinking about how you are breathing, take a minute and very silently invite the Holy Spirit to breathe in you. Invite him to dwell inside of you in a new way. Just pray, "Come, Holy Spirit." Pray it a few times. I dare you. It'll be a breath of fresh air. It will be a small taste of heaven.

Salvation Given

When he had said this, he breathed on them and said to them,
"Receive the Holy Spirit."
—JOHN 20:22

It was those stairs that reminded me of the Spirit; I guess you could say that it was a stairway to heaven.

THE BIBLE
AND THE
CATHOLIC
TRADITION

Christ said
"the Word,"
and the
Church began

For I long to see you, that I may impart to you some spiritual gift to strengthen you, that is, that we may be mutually encouraged by each other's faith, both yours and mine.

—ROMANS 1:11–12

"I don't feel like going to Mass; I don't get anything out of it." "Why do I have to sing?" "I don't have to go to church; I pray better by myself at home."

These are all popular excuses that most of us have either used or heard. Phrases like these point out that, for most people, there is Mass confusion (pun intended).

Solution Offered

At some point we've probably all heard the Holy Mass that we celebrate on Sundays also called a (Anyone?... Anyone?) liturgy.

What's a liturgy? One definition is that it's a "public work done in the service of another." That means that when you and I go to Mass, we're not just going for ourselves, to receive something. We're going for others, to give something.

Community is so important to the Mass. In fact, community is one of the four places we experience Christ in the Mass as Catholics (the other three being the Eucharist, the Word, and the priest).

St. Paul, in the above verse, is telling the Romans how much he'd like to see them, to pray with them, and to share the Eucharist and the Word with them. He understood the importance of community and the incredible effect that prayer with our brothers and sisters in Christ can have.

Reread this verse, however, and put God in the place of St. Paul. Listen to God's voice and hear what He's telling you and me today. This is an invitation to Mass, to adoration, to prayer.

Sometimes, I think, we just figure God isn't watching us, that he's too busy to pay attention to us unless we're talking to him (and sometimes we doubt it even then). The kicker is that God, since he is timeless, perfect, all-knowing, all-powerful, and so on, can never run out of room or attention for us. His network never goes down.

God is the Dad who loves to have his children come home and spend time with him, come around the table and eat. He isn't the dad who wants to see his kids for only one hour a week or during the holidays.

When's the last time you caught a daily Mass or went to adoration when you didn't have to or when it wasn't an organized prayer time? Find a half hour in your schedule this week, tell no one, and get there. Look at the verse below. Dad is longing to share something with us and to strengthen us.

Salvation Given

For I long to see you, that I may impart to you some spiritual gift to strengthen you, that is, that we may be mutually encouraged by each other's faith, both yours and mine.
—ROMANS 1:11–12

See ya at the dinner table.

You are what you eat.

> Now as they were eating, Jesus took bread, and blessed, and broke
> it, and gave it to the disciples and said, "Take, eat; this is my
> body."
>
> —MATTHEW 26:26

Is Jesus truly present in the Eucharist?

Solution Offered

One question: What did Jesus say?

Jesus is coming to your Church this Sunday, in the flesh (just like
every Sunday). He's not only asking you to believe, but inviting you to
experience heaven on earth. Yes, it defies all logic—God coming to us
in simple bread and wine. But then, Jesus defied all logic:

Jesus came to us not as a royal baby on a throne, but as a simple child
in a manger.

Jesus lived not as a powerful political ruler but as a common carpenter.

Jesus spread a message not of war and conquest but of peace and
forgiveness.

Jesus preached the gospel not just through words but also through
actions.

Jesus desired not to be served but to serve, washing the feet of the
apostles.

Jesus, the King, wore a crown not of gold but of thorns.

Jesus was elevated not in social stature but naked and bloodied upon
a cross.

Jesus was not buried with a royal procession but laid in a simple,
unmarked tomb.

Jesus comes to us at every Mass, not with bright lights and a big show but in simple bread and wine. Why? I like to think that it's because simple is Jesus's style.

If I were God, I wouldn't choose to come in bread and wine. But thank God I'm not God.

Bread and wine: If it's good enough for Jesus, it ought to be good enough for me. He said it, and I have no reason to doubt him. He's gotten me this far. Remember what the great author C. S. Lewis once wrote: "The command, after all, was, *'Take and eat,'* not *'take and understand.'*" Lord, I don't fully understand it, but I sure do appreciate it.

Whether you struggle with believing in the true presence of Christ or not, it never hurts to spend some time really thinking about it.

Pray for the faith this Sunday to see Jesus in the Eucharist in a new way. Continue to feed your faith and, in time, your doubts will starve to death.

Salvation Given

> Now as they were eating, Jesus took bread, and blessed, and broke it, and gave it to the disciples and said, "Take, eat; this is my body."
> —MATTHEW 26:26

If the people of Nazareth taught us anything, it's that Christ could be right in front of you and you might not recognize him.

I am with you always, to the close of the age.

—MATTHEW 28:20

Do you ever doubt that God exists? I mean, do you ever sit there at Mass and just think, "What if all of this is just made up? What if it's all fake? What if I'm going through all of this—trying to live according to what's right—and it's all a big lie?" If you have, you're like 90 percent of all Christians at one point or another (and the other 10 percent just don't admit it!).

Solution Offered

This verse is the very last sentence in the Gospel of St. Matthew, but it's one of the most important. You see, Matthew was writing to the Jewish people, and for years (thousands of years, actually) the Jews had been waiting for the Messiah. When the Messiah finally came—Jesus, that is—many followed him and believed, but many didn't. A lot of people had a hard time believing that Jesus was the Messiah, because they thought the Messiah would come out of the sky on a fiery chariot and cause the Romans (who were killing and persecuting Jews) to have, well, a really bad day.

Now, imagine you're an apostle, standing on a mountain. Jesus, whom you've followed and pledged your allegiance and life to, has died and risen. Think about that: He died, and he rose from the dead. But now he's ascending on a cloud right in front of you. He promises he'll never leave you. You've got to be thinking that some Cliff Notes would be great right now, because you can't figure out what's going on.

Remember, if Jesus were alive today, walking around in Jerusalem, CNN or Twitter or Instagram would report it. So the question arises,

"How could Jesus be with all of us until the end of time?" Yes, by the Holy Spirit, but more directly through the power of the Spirit. Yes, you got it: the Eucharist.

Over three hundred thousand times a day in our world, the Holy Mass is celebrated in countless languages and hundreds of countries, with the same exact readings and prayers. As Catholic Christians, you are part of something much bigger than yourselves, something with a rich history and a two thousand-year tradition. On Pentecost we celebrate the birthday of the Church, the day when the Holy Spirit blew the doors off the room where Christ's followers were assembled.

This Sunday at Mass, thank God for the gift of the Spirit, through whom we can always have Jesus in our midst. Look around and see Jesus not only in the Eucharist but also in the word in the readings, in the priest celebrating the Mass and speaking his words, and in the community of people around you, the body of Christ.

"I am with you always," he says. Believe it!

Salvation Given

I am with you always, to the close of the age.
—MATTHEW 28:20

Remember, when it comes to Church, you're never too bad to come in, and you're not too good to stay out.

The next sabbath almost the whole city gathered to hear the word
of God.

—ACTS 13:44

Have you ever been told that the Catholic Mass is not biblical? I was
talking to a really good friend the other day who told me, "The Catholic
Mass is absolutely unbiblical, and it focuses only on the 'priest' and 'the
bread wafers' and not on God's Word." Have you ever been faced with
a situation like this one?

Solution Offered

Did you know that the entire Mass from start to finish is completely
based on and founded in Scripture? Virtually every prayer and response
we say during the celebration of Mass is based on the Word of God.
Rather than beg you or anyone else to believe me, I'll give you just a
few examples:

In the name of the Father and of the Son and of the Holy Spirit.
(Matthew 28:19)

Amen. (1 Chronicles 16:36)

The grace of our Lord Jesus Christ, the love of God, and the communion of the Holy Spirit be with all of you. (2 Corinthians 13:13; NRSV)

The Lord be with you. (Ruth 2:4)

Glory to God in the highest, and on earth peace among men with
whom he is pleased. (Luke 2:14)

Blessed be God. (Psalm 68:35)

May the Lord accept the sacrifice at your hands. (Psalm 50:23)

Lift up your hearts; we lift them up to the Lord. (Lamentations 3:41)

Let us give thanks to the Lord our God. (Colossians 3:17)

Hosanna! Blessed is he who comes in the name of the Lord. (Mark 11:9–10)

Let us proclaim the mystery of our faith. (1 Timothy 3:16)

Christ has died, Christ is risen, Christ will come again. (1 Corinthians 15:3–5; Revelation 22:12)

From age to age you gathered your people to yourself, so that from the rising of the sun to its setting... (Psalm 103:17; 113:3)

Through him, with him, in him. (Romans 11:36)

This is the Lamb of God; happy are we who are called... (Revelation 19:9)

Hopefully you can now trust that a bunch of priests weren't sitting around a monastery a couple thousand years ago, making up random prayers for fun. Let's give the Holy Spirit some credit, huh?

Our Church, the universal (Catholic) faith—founded by Christ, led by the Spirit, and entrusted to Peter—is the oldest Christian religion. Our Mass, celebrated in countless languages around the world, hundreds of thousands of times a day, with the same readings, is totally, absolutely, unequivocally,

100 percent founded in Scripture.

Take pride in the fact that you're part of a long and glorious tradition, and be proud to be Catholic! The apostles were.

Salvation Given

The next sabbath almost the whole city gathered to hear the word of God.
—Acts 13:44

Go in peace to love and serve the Lord! (see Luke 7:50; 2 Chronicles 35:3)

> My lips will shout for joy,
>> when I sing praises to you;
>> my soul also, which you have rescued.
>
> —PSALM 71:23

How many languages do you speak? You might be surprised.

Solution Offered

It's amazing how many common phrases we still use today that come directly from God's Word. It hit me recently, though, how many foreign phrases we say at Mass that we might not know the meaning of. What struck me even more was how often I sing a response at Mass out of force of habit, without really pausing and praying those words.

These verses from the Psalms should really convict us that, when we are singing, it should never be just a response but a shout filled with joy. Singing invites, involves, and ignites our souls so that at Mass and in all our worship, singing is not merely a physical act, but a spiritual one.

Maybe you hear (or have heard) some of these phrases at your local church during Mass:

Agnus Dei
Miserere nobis
Dona nobis pacem
Kyrie eleison, Christe eleison

So maybe you've heard them. You might even be able to pronounce them…but what do they mean, really? Ask and ye shall receive.

Agnus Dei is Latin for "Lamb of God."

Miserere nobis is Latin for "have mercy on us."

Dona nobis pacem is Latin for "grant us peace."

Kyrie eleison is Greek for "Lord, have mercy."

Christe eleison is Greek for "Christ, have mercy."

Now, even if we already know the meanings, we should ask ourselves, "Are we simply responding to these phrases, or are we really praising and even "shouting out" to God (as this verse challenges us to do) with our whole heart?

When singing these words, we're not merely reciting some foreign or dead language; we're communicating in a spiritual way, begging the Lamb of God (Jesus) to have mercy on us (for our sins) and asking him to give us his grace and peace (of mind, heart, and soul).

These languages aren't dead, either, because if we are really praying them, they bring life. Thank God, too, that he is merciful—because when I sing out loud, I'll accept all the mercy I can get for my voice.

Salvation Given

My lips will shout for joy,
> when I sing praises to you;
> my soul also, which you have rescued.
—PSALM 71:23

Can I get an Amen? (Wait, we already covered that)

My son, do not regard lightly the discipline of the Lord,
nor lose courage…
For the Lord disciplines him whom he loves.
—HEBREWS 12:5–6

Ever get into trouble in church as a kid? I did—a lot.

Solution Offered

When I was still pretty little, there were several rules that my parents set for my brothers and sister and me before we entered Mass on Sunday.

Pay attention.

No talking, punching, pinching, shoving, slapping, or wet willies.

No toys that made noise.

No standing on the kneelers.

No fighting over who gets to put the money in the collection basket.

No trying to crush or break your brother's toes when putting the kneeler down (This rule had to be added following "the incident.")

No gum.

No crawling underneath the pew.

No trying to make your brother, the altar server, laugh.

And finally, certain brothers were never, under any circumstances, allowed to sit next to each other.

Now, these rules, for the most part, worked. They allowed everyone in our family and around us to actually hear what was being read, said, sung, and prayed at Mass. We knew that we had crossed a line either when my mother called us by our first and middle name or when my father stood up (and no one else in church did), took us by the arm, and walked us outside to have a…well…a "conversation."

Discipline. Through my father's disciplining us, we learned to discipline ourselves. That's love.

God loves us so much that he set up rules and guidelines to help us live every day, knowing that through discipline we would come to know, follow, and love him more deeply. My father never enjoyed pulling us out of church, but he did know a couple of things:

What was happening in God's house was important for us (and the people around us) to see and hear.

The same word in Latin that we get *discipline* from, we get *disciple* from.

I can't be a true disciple of Christ if I'm not disciplined in my prayer life, in reading my Bible, in attending Mass, in getting to reconciliation, in sharing the gospel, and in serving others. Discipline yourself in your faith journey, and embrace the loving discipline and structure that God the Father offers us daily and that Christ himself accepted.

Salvation Given

My son, do not regard lightly the discipline of the Lord,
nor lose courage…
For the Lord disciplines him whom he loves.
—HEBREWS 12:5–6

Thanks for looking out for me, Dad (Abba).

A leper came to him beseeching him, and kneeling said to him, "If you will, you can make me clean." Moved with pity, he stretched out his hand and touched him, and said to him, "I will; be clean."
—Mark 1:40–41

Every Sunday, millions of people enter Catholic churches around the world. We bless ourselves with holy water, greet one another (hopefully), spot an empty seat, and before we sit, we (hopefully) genuflect (kneel on one knee) to Jesus, present in the tabernacle. Why?

Solution Offered

The phrase "kneeling down" in some Bible translations is written "on bended knee," which is written *genu flexo* in Latin. Does that term look familiar? *Genu flexo* or "genuflect."

You see, the leper from the passage quoted above kneels before Christ as a sign of honor, worship, and respect, uttering his faith in Jesus's ability to heal him. This is a biblical example of why we are expected to genuflect when we pass by the tabernacle (if it's located in the church) and when we are before the Blessed Sacrament. We are just like the leper, in need of Jesus's healing. We bend on one knee to show Jesus, who is truly present in the Eucharist, our honor for him.

Unfortunately, nowadays, not as many people genuflect when entering the pew before Mass, and few people show Christ the respect he deserves when passing by the tabernacle. A lot of people just don't know—a fact that those of us who do know need to get better at sharing with others.

I've often heard people say that we don't need to genuflect because Christ is present in the community assembled and in the Word.

According to this line of reasoning, we would need to genuflect to everyone in church if we wanted to show Christ honor. While it is true that Christ is present within us, it is a mistake to consider that presence equal to Christ's true and unique presence in the Eucharist.

Some folks say that a bow is just as good as taking a knee. There are a lot of reasons why the Church says we should bend at the knee instead, but to put it simply, a bow doesn't say what genuflecting says.

Sometimes we also bow to people, but to get down on our knees—now that is a gesture that is reserved for God. The psalmist says not just that we should "bow down" before God, but that we should "kneel before the Lord our Maker" (see Psalm 95:6).

This might seem minor to some of us, others of us might forget, and still others might not have learned the habit of genuflecting when passing before Jesus in the Eucharist. If you fit in any of these categories, don't be mad at yourself. But be aware now. Let those around you see the belief and the reverence you have for Jesus, truly present in the Eucharist.

Salvation Given

> A leper came to him beseeching him, and kneeling said to him, "If you will, you can make me clean." Moved with pity, he stretched out his hand and touched him, and said to him, "I will; be clean."
> —MARK 1:40–41

A woman at my parish is 102 years old, and she still genuflects. That's not easy at her age. Think about it. Actions follow beliefs.

Getting back at God with the voice he gave me.

David and all Israel danced before God with all their might, singing to the accompaniment of lyres, harps, tambourines, cymbals, trumpets.

—1 CHRONICLES 13:8, JB

What is your normal experience at Mass? Does Mass usually start at ten o'clock sharp and end at eleven o'clock dull? Have you ever wanted to scream at Mass because a lot of the people just aren't into it? What are you called to do at Mass?

Solution Offered

So today we have this verse from 1 Chronicles (which isn't exactly a book anybody reads every day), and we have an incredible example of a disciple of God.

Here's David—King David, the most powerful man in Israel at the time—*dancing* and *singing* with great enthusiasm. Let me write that again, because it's just that important. King David, leader of all Israel, was so overcome with enthusiasm and love for God that he sang and danced before God. Now, that's joy—that's passion.

Is that how you feel when you're before God during the celebration of the Holy Mass? When you look upon Christ in the Eucharist and encounter Christ in the readings, do you stop to think about how cool it is that you are experiencing God, the Creator of the universe—of the earth, the heavens, and you and me?

Notice two things here: First, David didn't care what people thought. He was celebrating God's existence and God's love for him. Second, David was a leader in love with God who led others by his example. It says in the verse that all of Israel joined in the dancing.

We as Catholics were fortunate to have a leader like that in St. John Paul II. He was passionately in love with God, and he led us by an incredible example. His enthusiasm for the Lord and his people was contagious. Countless had their hearts turned back to God through his pontificate and life...not bad for a poor young (almost) orphan born into a war-torn country.

Start praying today, and pray every day this week, that this Sunday you will have a new passion for God. It may mean that you will need to sing louder, or sit away from distractions—maybe even in one of the first couple of pews. Do whatever it takes to put yourself in a position to get more out of Mass this weekend and to lead others by your passionate participation. You don't have to be jumping up and down (that could be dangerous), but you are called to full, conscious, active participation.

Catholicism is not a spectator sport.

Salvation Given

David and all Israel danced before God with all their might, singing to the accompaniment of lyres, harps, tambourines, cymbals, trumpets.

—1 CHRONICLES 13:8, JB

Why do we fight for front row seats at concerts but sit in the back at church?

Lord, give me the desire to be a front-row Catholic.

> For all the promises of God find their Yes in him. That is why we
> utter the Amen through him, to the glory of God.
>
> —2 CORINTHIANS 1:20

Do you ever speak without thinking? (Wait, think before you answer.)
Do you ever say something before you really stop to think about what it
means? (Are you two-for-two on this quiz so far?) Me, too.

Solution Offered

In the Gospel of Matthew, Jesus says the word *Amen* about thirty times.

In the course of a normal Sunday Mass, we say or sing the word
Amen between ten and twenty times.

Amen is a derivative of the Hebrew word *aman*, which means "to
confirm" or "to strengthen." When we say "Amen," we are proclaiming
something. We are professing our strongest belief, with all of our
Christian soul. We are saying, "Yes, I believe!"

Not me. I can honestly say that most of the time when I say "Amen,"
I'm not stopping to think about what I'm saying. I usually say it as more
of a reaction than a prayerful response, as a way of kind of ending a
prayer and moving on.

Well, that changes today.

When I finish making the Sign of the Cross, I'm gonna proclaim,
"Amen!"—sort of like a spiritual high five to God, telling him, "I'm
right here with ya, Big Guy, and you can count on me, because I do
believe."

When the entire church erupts into the Great Amen at Mass this
weekend, I'm gonna sing it so loud that the person next to me will
think I have a screw loose. And when I proceed forward to encounter

and receive our Lord in His Most Holy Eucharist, and the Eucharistic minister says to me, "The Body of Christ," my Amen response will be strong and determined. My Amen will leave no doubt in anyone who hears me that I belong to Christ, that I am proud to be a Catholic, and that I believe in him. I have met him in his sacraments, in his Word, and in his children here on earth.

Who's with me?

Let's never again allow our Amen to be a reaction instead of a response.

Salvation Given

For all the promises of God find their Yes in him. That is why we utter the Amen through him, to the glory of God.

—2 CORINTHIANS 1:20

Amen?

For something that's stained, it sure is beautiful.

While you have the light, believe in the light, so that you may become children of light.

—JOHN 12:36, NRSV

What is the purpose of the stained glass windows in church? Ever think about it?

In case you've never heard the following story, I wanted to share it with you.

Solution Offered

It was Sunday morning, and as always, a young family made their way into Mass. A beautiful little six-year-old girl, the youngest, sat amazed, gazing up at the ceilings, the candles, the statues, and the crucifix.

Then she noticed an incredible array of colored light beaming onto the floor in front of her. Her eyes immediately scaled the walls to find the source. She saw the brilliant, early morning sun shining through the stained-glass window.

She asked her father, "Daddy, who are those people in the colored windows?"

"Those are the saints, sweetheart, people who lived for God and who loved him very much."

The young girl nodded in approval. She kept her eyes glued to the stained glass for the remainder of the Mass.

A couple of years later the same girl sat in her Catholic elementary school religion class. "Who are the saints?" the teacher asked the students at the beginning of the lesson. No one in class raised a hand, with the exception of the little girl. The teacher called on her, and she humbly rose to answer the question. "So, who are the saints?" the teacher asked again.

"The saints are the ones the light shines through," the little girl innocently replied.

Remember, the saints were ordinary people who got tired, who got hungry, who even got annoyed. They got sick, they got headaches, they made mistakes, they sinned, and they went through temptations, too—just like you and me. They dealt with the same types of situations, people, and annoyances that you and I struggle with every day. The big difference is how they responded to God's call and how they chose to live in the midst of hardship.

You can be a saint. I could be a saint. We are all called to be saints. Don't ever think, "That could never be me." It can be you; "with God nothing will be impossible" (Luke 1:37).

Start today. Smile. Serve. Affirm. Let the joy of Christ radiate within you. Really try, in a new way, to allow the light of Christ, the awesomeness of God, to shine through you—to the wonder and amazement of all who see it.

That would be a beautiful gift, one that shouldn't be reserved just for church.

Salvation Given

While you have the light, believe in the light, so that you may become children of light.
—JOHN 12:36, NRSV

Make your life a stained-glass work of art to a world in need of more beauty.

Now the birth of Jesus the Messiah took place in this way. When his mother Mary had been engaged to Joseph, but before they lived together, she was found to be with child from the Holy Spirit. Her husband Joseph her, being a righteous man...
—MATTHEW 1:18–19, NRSV

Do you act like your father? Jesus did.

Solution Offered

Just because St. Joseph is not mentioned enough times to fill up even one page of Scripture, that does not mean he was not extremely important (heck, Pontius Pilate was barely even mentioned, but he wound up being pretty significant).

The fact is that while Jesus's earthly father, St. Joseph, may not have been mentioned frequently, his fingerprints are all over the Gospel stories because his life echoes through Christ. Through the man that Jesus became, we have a window into the man our Lord's earthly father (St. Joseph) really was.

So, what do we know about the man whom God entrusted to raise his only Son?

Joseph was a humble man with his feet on the ground, not with his head in the clouds. He is described as righteous, meaning he was a respectful, obedient, humble man of integrity who knew the law and (more importantly) followed it. He was human, not perfect. He was merciful. Simple and holy like his wife, Mary, Joseph must have been very down to earth. That does tend to make sense, since the very words *humble* and *human* both come from the Latin root word *humus*, which literally means "ground."

It's fascinating, too, to note that the Bible does not mention anyone else at the scene during Jesus's birth. Back then, it would have been customary for another woman, a relative or close family friend (called a "midwife"), to be at Mary's side during the childbirth, helping her through it and delivering the baby. No such woman is mentioned, though; the only other person we know for a fact to be there is Joseph. Joseph was not only there when Jesus was born…he probably even delivered the baby King. That's right, he delivered the deliverer.

We know that Joseph was a hard worker; in fact, the term "carpenter" probably isn't the best translation, since the actual word in Greek means Joseph was not just a carpenter with wood, but an artisan with all kinds of materials, including marble and stone. Joseph would have been skilled with his hands, was very strong, worked mostly outdoors, and was no stranger to manual labor. Many artisans and craftsmen at the time would have worked on boats and bigger ships, but living in Nazareth, Joseph most likely wouldn't have done much of that. Historians and scholars tend to agree that Joseph would have spent time working on farming equipment (like yokes), on furniture and tools used in homes, and on other large outdoor structures like amphitheaters, meeting areas, and palaces. In fact, after Jesus turned twelve, he would have been at Joseph's side every day, watching, learning, and eventually working on projects alongside his dad.

Joseph is often overlooked because of the lack of details and the infrequency of direct references. The fact remains, though, that God entrusted his only Son to this man. Like Mary, it's not like God is going to let just anyone raise the most important person this world has ever known. Joseph must be one of the finest men to ever walk the face of this planet. Joseph was so important and so special to God that God contacted him three different times with messages and instructions through angels.

Joseph was a model of true humility and love. He loved God enough to accept the role he was given. He loved Mary enough to protect her and provide for her. He was the first man to hold Jesus the night of his birth. Growing up, the first person Jesus ever referred to as Abba was probably St. Joseph. Through the sacrifice and self-control he showed in his marriage, he further demonstrated his manhood. He is the kind of man that every man should aspire to be and that every woman should seek to marry.

Joseph wasn't perfect. He was humble. He was hardworking. He was open. He loved God, Mary, and Jesus. Joseph was a man after God's own heart.

Salvation Given

Now the birth of Jesus the Messiah took place in this way. When his mother Mary had been engaged to Joseph, but before they lived together, she was found to be with child from the Holy Spirit. Her husband Joseph her, being a righteous man...
—MATTHEW 1:18–19, NRSV

St. Joseph, pray for us that we might know Jesus as well as you did and seek to have him at our side as you had him at yours.

For where two or three are gathered in my name, there am I in the midst of them.

—Matthew 18:20

Do any famous people go to your church?

I received a phone call last week from a friend of mine—we'll call him Tim—who works for a local TV news station. He wanted to do a story on all of the people "returning to God and filling churches because of the negative state of the world, the down economy, threats of terrorism, increased disease, etc."

"Great idea," I told him.

"Now, does your church get really big crowds?" he asked. "Because we want to get good shots with the camera. Oh, and are there any famous people who go there?"

"Do you mean besides God?" I responded.

"C'mon, Mark, you know what I mean," he replied.

"And you know what I mean, Tim," I said.

You see, Tim and I were in the same youth group, and we used to talk about God all the time. But at some point (like so many others we care about), he just stopped coming to church. So when he called and asked to do the story, I had to just look up to the sky, smile, and laugh, because I felt like God was giving me another chance with Tim. (God is good that way.) I decided to take this opportunity to make him think about his question in a new way.

"Famous people? You want famous people?" I asked him.

"Yeah, the more the better," he replied.

"Well, I'd be happy to introduce you to the Blessed Virgin Mary, St. Francis, St. Thérèse, St. Maximilian Kolbe, St. Maria Goretti, St. Jerome, and St. Paul, for starters. They, along with the rest of the communion of saints, are at each and every Mass, and I usually ask them to sit next to me and pray with me. I'm sure they'd scoot down the pew and make some room for you."

He laughed, and we talked a little bit. He was beginning to get it. That Sunday he came and did the story, and we had a great conversation afterwards. In fact, he came to church again the following weekend.

While all stories don't end up like this, some do, and other stories still might.

There are a lot of people, even Catholics who go to Mass religiously (pun intended), who aren't "into it" because they do not understand fully what's going on. You and I can change that, by striving to learn more about why we do what we do at Mass.

There's plenty of space at God's dining room table (altar). Now all people need is the invitation. Have you sent yours out? I've been a little lazy myself lately, but that's all gonna change.

Salvation Given

> For where two or three are gathered in my name, there am I in the midst of them.
> —MATTHEW 18:20

Jesus—he's there every week. And that's why I am, too.

It doesn't hurt anyone but me.

> If any one has caused pain, he has caused it not to me, but in
> some measure…to you all.
>
> —2 CORINTHIANS 2:5

Who do my sins hurt? Who do your sins hurt? Only you? A popular misconception is that our sins hurt only us. It's common for me to hear someone say, "What's the big deal with (blank)? I'm only hurting myself." OK, I'll say this as lovingly as I can: "That's a crock!" Sin runs deeper than that.

Solution Offered

You know, at the beginning of Mass we say, as a community, "I confess to Almighty God, *and to you, my brothers and sisters*, that I have greatly sinned." Ever notice that we're admitting wrongdoing not only to God but also to the community of believers assembled with us?

Did you know that the sacrament of reconciliation didn't always take place in a safe little confessional box? No, it was far more public and far more embarrassing, but people confessed, anyway. Why you may ask? What the people back then realized—that we don't realize now or don't want to admit that we realize—is that sin hurts everyone. When I sin, it doesn't just hurt me; it hurts others, some whom I know about and some whom I don't.

Have you ever sat in the nonsmoking section near the smoking section? Sin can be like secondhand smoke. The sinner might not realize or admit that his or her smoke is having an effect on others. Those inhaling the smoke may or may not realize it, but the smoke does have an unhealthy effect. You see, once the smoke (sin) is out there, there's no way to control its effects or its harm to other people.

I have had a number of friends who think that if they smoked out, or drank, or whatever, those decisions and their consequences stopped with them. That's not the case. We are all one body, those who realize it and those who don't. Our actions, good or bad, affect other people. All of our actions matter.

I took a hard look at my own life recently to see if any of my own secondhand sin might be making others' faith walks more difficult. The answer was yes, and I've had to make some tough changes. But by the grace of God and prayers from fellow Christians, like you, I continue to get better.

How about you? Any changes needed?

Know this, at the very least: I am praying for you. That I promise.

Salvation Given

If any one has caused pain, he has caused it not to me, but in some measure…to you all.

—2 CORINTHIANS 2:5

Sometimes we forget that sin really is optional.

A leper came to him beseeching him, and kneeling said to him, "If you will, you can make me clean." Moved with pity, he stretched out his hand and touched him, and said to him, "I will; be clean."
—MARK 1:40–41

You shower every day (hopefully), so you're probably clean, but is your car clean right now? How often do you wash the car or get it washed? Do you ever just wait to wash it because it's just going to keep getting dirty or because it's going to rain soon? I do.

Solution Offered

After I wash my car, I am so careful about where and how I drive. It's spotless and shiny, reflecting the sunlight (hopefully blinding the birds above who normally treat it as a target), and I want to keep it that way. I avoid construction zones. I avoid dirt roads. I watch out for mud. I go around corners more slowly so that rainwater doesn't splash up and dirty my car even the smallest amount.

Once I get some dirt on it though, all bets are off. I'm going through construction sites, I'm hitting puddles, off-roading through mud bogs—I mean, who cares? I might even think about washing it and then say, "What's the point? It'll just get dirty again."

It's the same with my soul. Once I've reconciled with God and have gone to confession, my soul is like my clean car: spotless, shiny, reflecting the true Son light. And I am so careful to keep it that way. I watch my language closely; I think before I speak; I avoid the puddles of sin at every turn.

Once I go through a puddle, though, boy, it gets easier and easier to sin. "It's already dirty," I say to myself. Then when I think about going to confession (but don't really want to go), I say to myself, "Self, it's just gonna get dirty again," and I allow that to stop me from going.

Do you think that's what Jesus would say? It's not. Jesus wants our souls to be clean. He doesn't care if we go to the car wash of confession every day; he'd rather have us do that than drive around the car *he* created with mud all over it. Jesus wants all of us to be made clean. It is God's greatest desire to have us with him, back home, in heaven.

At the same time, not everyone is getting into heaven. That's not a popular thing to say today, because a lot of people think it's not nice to say that some folks aren't getting into heaven. To them I say, "Sorry, folks, I'm just quoting Jesus" (see Matthew 22:14; 25:33, 46).

Salvation Given

> A leper came to him beseeching him, and kneeling said to him, "If you will, you can make me clean." Moved with pity, he stretched out his hand and touched him, and said to him, "I will; be clean."
> —MARK 1:40–41

Heaven's parking lot is full of shiny cars. And there's a space waiting for you.

Jesus said to them again, "Peace be with you. As the Father has sent me, even so I send you." And when he had said this, he breathed on them, and said to them, "Receive the Holy Spirit. If you forgive the sins of any, they are forgiven; if you retain the sins of any, they are retained."

—JOHN 20:21–23

Why do Catholics have to go to a priest to be forgiven? Have you ever been asked that? Why can't we just think about what we did wrong and say we're sorry in our minds, by ourselves?

Solution Offered

Think about confession for a second. Why would God want to humble us so badly by making us share our faults and sins with another person? Now read the above verse again.

Do you see how Jesus gives his apostles, the first members of Christ's sacramental priesthood, the power to forgive or not to forgive? This is vital for understanding reconciliation.

Say that you work at a remote gas station and a car (without GPS) pulls in to ask for directions. Now, when the driver gets out, how do you know what directions to give? How do you know whether to tell him he's on the right road or the wrong road? Do you just guess where he wants to go based on looking at the guy, or do you listen to him first?

It's the same way with a priest during the sacrament of reconciliation. By necessity, a priest can know whether to forgive sins or retain them (as this verse from St. John affirms) only once he has heard them. Hearing the sins is essential.

But we still have the question of why go to a priest in the first place. Some of you might say that a priest can't forgive sins anyway; only God can do that.

Well, we need to understand the role of the priest in confession. We aren't confessing our sins to the priest, but to God. The priest is acting *in persona Christi*, which is a big way of saying, "in the person of Christ." At that moment in confession, through the sacramental grace and power of the priest's ordination, the priest is standing in the physical place of Jesus. That's why the priest says, "I absolve you," and not, "Jesus absolves you." (It's the same during the consecration at Mass, when the priest says, "This is my body," not, "This is his body," or, "This is Jesus's body.")

Reconciliation is offered at about 90 percent of all Catholic churches on Saturday afternoons. Consider this a gentle reminder from your big brother, Mark.

I say it because I love you, but not at much as he does.

Salvation Given

Jesus said to them again, "Peace be with you. As the Father has sent me, even so I send you." And when he had said this, he breathed on them, and said to them, "Receive the Holy Spirit. If you forgive the sins of any, they are forgiven; if you retain the sins of any, they are retained."
—JOHN 20:21–23

Forgiveness is always free, but that doesn't mean that confession is always easy.
—E.W. LUTZER

DEALING WITH LIFE'S TEMPTATIONS AND TRIALS

The high road
to heaven
has its
potholes

Does Life Seem Tough?

"Hey, God, ease up!"

God is faithful, and he will not let you be tempted beyond your strength, but with the temptation will also provide the way of escape, that you may be able to endure it.

—1 CORINTHIANS 10:13

Have you ever thought that God makes life too difficult? Think about it. Think about all those times you've been really tempted and have fallen because the temptation was too great. Think about all those days when nothing seemed to go right and you wondered, "God, why are you doing this to me?" When's the last time you had a day like that? Maybe even today...

Solution Offered

First of all, as Christians we need to realize that there's a big difference between trials and temptations. Trials come from God, but temptations come from the devil and from within. How do we know?

Read the Scripture verse again. God does not want us to fail. He would never set us up to fail. That means that all those times we say, "It was too hard," after we've sinned, what happened wasn't God's fault but ours. This passage from Corinthians reminds us that God will never put us in a situation that we can't handle or survive, as long as (and here's the kicker) we have the courage and the humility to call on him.

Obviously, if you're reading this book, you take an active role in your faith. Just as obviously, another weekend is coming up. A lot of Fridays and Saturdays offer us more difficult situations to respond to than the other days of the week. Fridays and Saturdays, too, have a funny way of revealing what we really believe about the God of our Sundays.

If you're confronted with a trial this weekend, have the courage to call on God, and he'll give you what you need to get through it. If you find yourself in a tempting situation, realize that it isn't God setting you up to fail. Live for Jesus in that situation, take pride in your faith and in calling yourself a Catholic Christian, kick the devil in the rear, and tell him that he can't win because you stand with Christ.

Salvation Given

God is faithful, and he will not let you be tempted beyond your strength, but with the temptation will also provide the way of escape, that you may be able to endure it.
—1 CORINTHIANS 10:13

Be proud of Jesus Christ. He's proud of you.

We also boast in our sufferings, knowing that suffering produces endurance, and endurance produces character, and character produces hope, and hope does not disappoint us, because God's love has been poured into our hearts through the Holy Spirit that has been given to us.

—ROMANS 5:3–5

If God is so loving, why do we suffer?

Solution Offered

Suffering does not make sense to this modern world. Not even the most scientifically astute minds or advanced mathematical theorems can explain the purpose of suffering. Science cannot give us an answer, so technology attempts to give us hundreds of ways to avoid it. That's part of the problem…not suffering, but avoidance. Suffering to a non-Christian mind is pointless, but to a Christian, suffering is nothing short of perfecting love.

I know, it doesn't seem to make sense, right? How can love be rooted in suffering? How can pain be a good thing? Look at a pregnant woman in her third trimester, and you have your answer: It's all about perspective. The perspective, the answer to the question and problem of suffering, is at the heart of the above verse from Romans.

The truth is that suffering can be a beautiful thing, if we have the courage to trust God with everything, like Jesus did upon the cross. It was in my greatest moments of suffering…true suffering…that I learned not that God had abandoned me but, rather, how much God really loves me. God, in his love, allows us to suffer from time to time, not because he dislikes us, but because he loves us that much. When we suffer, we don't just come to understand the pain of Christ's cross more, we come to understand the depth of God's love for us: that he would endure such pain for us—in our place. We have a God who endured death so we would never have to do so.

We have a God who would rather die than risk spending eternity without us.

Some of the suffering we go through is a result of our own sinful decisions and actions. God never wants that for us, obviously; it was our own doing. There are other sufferings God allows, however, that are not due to our sin. Others' divorce, disease, natural disasters, and so on are examples of suffering that is out of our control but that our Lord might allow for a time. When we go through pain it is easy to feel abandoned or forgotten, but suffering doesn't mean God doesn't love us, He does. Even Jesus suffered, and he was completely without sin.

It's through suffering that we grow in endurance, character, and ultimately, in hope, as we learn from this passage in Romans. Our suffering is not without value if we know Jesus. When you are suffering, you can pray and unite your sufferings to the only one who truly loves you perfectly or knows all you are feeling. When you go to Jesus, you're not going to a God who only knows heaven; instead, you're placing your hurting heart into pierced hands that understand both the pain of suffering and the glory of redemption.

Our suffering is forever bound to his. It is in Christ's brokenness that he saves us. It is in our brokenness that we, in turn, can help him save others through us. If those who profess to know and love God (you and I) go through hardships, all the while refusing to take our eyes off of our Creator, especially in moments of intense loneliness or pain...how much stronger will those around us become? How much stronger will our witness be? How many more of our friends and family will want to come to know our source of strength and of joy in the face of trial or pain?

For you and I are the body of Christ, broken and shared so that others might live…just like the Eucharist. Every one of the tears I have ever shed has, in time, helped another. If my brokenness can bring hope or comfort, wisdom or counsel, peace or even joy to another member of God's family, then that pain was not worthless but very worthwhile. Never waste your pain. Pray to God, offer it up to him as a prayer for someone else who is in pain, and turn that sorrow into something worthwhile.

If I am a true Christian, I don't view things the same way a non-Christian does. Someone who doesn't know Jesus views this world as an ending place; Christians see it as a preparation place. Someone who doesn't believe in Christ will probably never understand the purpose of suffering, but a Christian knows the end of the story. Suffering is nothing less than participating in the perfect "love triangle" of the Blessed Trinity.

Our suffering thrusts us deep into the heart of the Trinity, the most complete and true form of love that exists. The love between God the Father and God the Son is a love so selfless and so real that it has to be expressed in its own complete person, the third person of the Trinity, the Holy Spirit.

Pain is temporary, but victory is forever. Suffering lasts a short time, but the joy of Christ is eternal. Don't believe me? Just ask a mother moments after giving birth. Suffering brings life to life in a newer, more profound way. Like life, suffering is a mystery, designed to point us back to our Creator.

Suffering is not a waste of time; it is a moment in time. Suffering does not sever your relationship with God but more deeply unites you to him.

We also boast in our sufferings, knowing that suffering produces endurance, and endurance produces character, and character produces hope, and hope does not disappoint us, because God's love has been poured into our hearts through the Holy Spirit that has been given to us.

—ROMANS 5:3–5

Don't close your eyes to the crucifixion, or you'll miss the resurrection.

More or less, everything.

> And this is my prayer, that your love may overflow more and
> more with knowledge and full insight.
> —Philippians 1:9, NRSV

What are you looking for in life?

Some people want to be taller, some smaller, some heavier, some skinnier. Some folks want to be smarter, some funnier, some richer, some simpler. Some souls want to be happier, some want more friends, some want to live longer.

Everyone wants to be loved. How many, though, want to love better?

Solution Offered

This is one of those really interesting Scripture passages. It gets to the core of humanity pretty quickly, stating that our goal should not be for earthly possessions or titles, but for greater love, both given and received.

I have so many areas that I need and want to grow in. I have so much room to grow as a Catholic Christian. I have so much learning to do if I really want to grow in knowledge.

I have a long way to go in my growth in holiness.

And God is good with that. He's OK with my baby steps as long as they are in a forward direction. He wants that kind of growth for us; that's what this verse is telling us. He wants good things for us, yes, but he wants everything to start with love. He wants us to learn how to more perfectly love, beginning with loving him, next loving the person he created in you, and then continuing with the people he places around you in your family, friends, and community. If you don't learn how to love God and to love yourself, how will you ever be able to properly love those around you?

I got to thinking, and personally I can begin better loving God by:

- Thinking about others more and myself less.
- Affirming others more and tearing them down less.
- Leading others more and following less.
- Talking to God more and on my cell phone less.
- Praying for others more and for myself less.
- Serving other more and serving myself less.
- Listening to others more and talking less.
- Reading Scripture more and watching television less.

So what is stopping me? Nothing is stopping me...except me. Have you noticed that this verse is a prayer? Read it again. This is St. Paul's prayer! It should be ours, too. Our prayer should be that our love for God (and for each other) increases not only in all perception but also in knowledge.

If only there were a book I could read to teach me how to grow in knowledge and in love of God and neighbor. Hmm, where might I find such a divinely inspired book? Where, oh where might it exist? Oh, if only such a book existed.

Oh, right...

Salvation Given

And this is my prayer, that your love may overflow more and more with knowledge and full insight.

—PHILIPPIANS 1:9, NRSV

Do you love God? More or less?

So I find it to be a law that when I want to do right, evil lies close
at hand.

—ROMANS 7:21

Do you believe in the devil? Are you scared of the devil? God isn't
scared of the devil, and as his children, we have nothing to fear either.

The Bible tells us the final score. Thanks to Jesus, we win and the
devil loses. That's why he's called "Lose-ifer."

Solution Offered

When I was in high school, I didn't believe in the devil. When I screwed
up, I didn't want to blame anyone but myself. I used to think that I
should be mature enough to take all the blame.

Let me tell you, I don't think that way anymore. There are a couple
of things I've learned about the devil that we all need to know and
remember:

Satan does exist.

The greatest thing that the devil has ever accomplished is making us,
you and me, believe that he doesn't exist. That way our defenses are
down and we're easier targets.

Given these two facts, what is St. Paul telling the Romans? The devil
keeps very busy, and the devil does not waste time. It's when you're
getting closer to God that the devil works harder on you. That's why St.
Paul says, "Evil lies close at hand."

If you're being tempted a lot in your life, that means that you make
the devil nervous. It means that you're putting effort into your faith,
and that's bad for the little lyin', back-stabbin', smack-talkin', guilt-
givin', horn-headed, pitchfork-holdin' punk.

Be honest with yourself. What areas of your life are you weakest in? The areas that you are weakest in are the first areas that the devil's gonna take a shot at. Sin most commonly enters through those tiny doors that we intentionally leave open. Identify those areas, and pray about them. Turn them over to God, and let Jesus in.

Eternity is a long time. No, let me rephrase that: Eternity is a long, long, long, long, long, long time. The devil wants you to focus on right now, not eternity. He'll even try to make you doubt heaven exists. Well, heaven does exist, and God wants you there!

The devil is gonna do everything to keep you out of heaven. Every time you're tempted, don't just look at the right decision as a way to make God happy. Look at it as a chance to show the devil that he doesn't have a shot at you. You're better than that, and you're stronger than that.

And you're worth more than you know. Your soul was purchased with Jesus's blood, and your love for God is your thanks.

God believes in you, and so do I.

Salvation Given

So I find it to be a law that when I want to do right, evil lies close at hand.

—ROMANS 7:21

The devil is a loser.

For he will command his angels concerning you

TO GUARD YOU IN ALL YOUR WAYS.

On their hands they will bear you up.

—Psalm 91:11–12

Is your guardian angel in good shape? Do you keep them busy? I do.

Solution Offered

I have a friend who is such a klutz. He is always tripping or falling over things; he is constantly hurting himself. We used to laugh about how his guardian angel must drink a lot of coffee to constantly be alert and how he should get paid overtime by God.

Obviously angels don't have physical bodies and never sleep (they're good that way), but let's not ruin the joke by injecting too much theology. Oh wait, too late.

This verse from the Psalms is one of the main verses used to explain guardian angels (you can also check out Matthew 18:10 and Exodus 23:20–23) and to remind us that angels are very real, they do exist, and they are among God's absolute greatest gifts to us. Angels are constantly around us and beside us. Angels play significant roles throughout God's plan of salvation. Think about it:

An angel stopped Abraham before he killed his son, Isaac.

An angel passed over Egypt, allowing for Moses and the Jews to escape.

An angel announced God's hope and plan to the Virgin Mary.

An angel calmed Joseph's fears about taking Mary as his wife.

An angel was at the empty tomb, announcing Jesus's resurrection.

An angel (St. Michael the Archangel) kicked Satan's pointy tail.

Angels are alive and at work in our lives. In fact, angels are mentioned almost three hundred times throughout the Bible. So what do we know about angels from Sacred Scripture? Glad you asked.

Angels are created by God. (Ephesians 3:9)

Angels report directly to God. (Job 1:6)

Angels possess free will. (Jude 1:6)

Angels have the mission to serve, worship, and glorify God. (Revelation 4:8)

Angels are spiritual beings, not human beings. (Hebrews 1:14)

Angels are mighty (Psalm 103:20) and wise. (Daniel 9:21–22)

Angels don't know everything. (Matthew 24:36)

Think about it, angels are just one more way God loves us and watches out for us. While we aren't angels, nor will we become angels, we are like angels in a few ways: we come from God, we are important to God, and we exist to serve God. Oh, and when we pray at Mass, we are surrounded by and singing alongside the angels—but they never sing off-key.

Salvation Given

For he will command his angels concerning you

to guard you in all your ways.

On their hands they will bear you up.

—PSALM 91:11–12

Picture angels surrounding your bed every night—there to pray and sing, there to guard and fight.

Be still, and know that I am God.

—PSALM 46:10

Do you have a lot of stress in your life? Do you ever get scared when you think about the future or get worried when you look at the present? Do you ever look up at the clouds, shake your head, and ask, "Why?"

Solution Offered

This is one of my favorite verses in all of the Bible. I like to think of myself as a fairly laid-back person, yet so often I find myself allowing things of the world, situations that I have no control over, to worry me or stress me out. After a while, if I let them, these situations can really get me down and make me forget the Good News of the gospel.

Now, do I mean that we should skip up and down the streets, holding hands, carrying flowers, and singing "Kumbaya" or "On Eagles' Wings"? No, not at all (that is, unless you want everyone, myself included, to make fun of you).

It's OK to be concerned about situations in our lives. We're human. Whether you're struggling in school or in a relationship, having a hard time at work or at home, no matter how little or great the problem is, God is in control. He can handle it.

Whatever situation in your life has you at all worried, don't. Today God reminds us that sometimes we just need to pray and to trust. I mean what I say…er…write:

Worry will drive you and me crazy. We're talkin' gray hair, lost hair, high blood pressure, premature wrinkles, ulcers…

Concern will drive us to our knees—to our knees in prayer.

Take the situation that makes you most concerned, and offer it up to God.

Salvation Given

Be still, and know that I am God.
—PSALM 46:10

Remember the two eternal truths:

1. There is a God.
2. You're not him.

For this commandment which I command you this day is not too
hard, neither is it far off for you.

—DEUTERONOMY 30:11

Where do you see God at work in your life? If you don't, you're not
looking hard enough. Take a serious look at your life today, or this
month, or this year. God is and has been at work, in your life and in
mine.

So where do you see God at work in your life?

Solution Offered

Have you ever heard that the Lord works in mysterious ways? I have,
and although sometimes God does work mysteriously, I also believe
that sometimes God is obvious.

No, I mean really obvious. No, we're talkin' "couldn't be clearer if a
lightning bolt hit me between the eyes" obvious or "couldn't be more
obvious if a voice spoke out of the clouds" kind of obvious.

Speaking for myself, a lot of the time I make things more difficult
than they need to be. Sometimes, because I'm stubborn or because I
want things my way, I ignore really obvious decisions in my life that
need to be made, and I refuse to put God first.

I used to focus on situations in my life that took my eyes off Jesus or
my attention away from God, and I would try to justify them. I used
to allow myself to be in tempting situations and think I would not be
affected. Yeah, right!

Finally I admitted that God spoke to me very obviously—through
the priest at my parish, for instance. He told me things I didn't want
to hear. Through him, God told me things I needed to hear, for my

own spiritual good. Then I started noticing God's voice in my youth minister, in my teachers, in my parents, in all kinds of people who loved me enough to speak the truth to me, the truth of Christ.

What situations and relationships in your life pull you away from God? Are you willing to make difficult decisions, even sever unhealthy relationships?

Listen to the words from Deuteronomy. God is not nearly as "far off" as he is obvious. Let's be honest with ourselves, step up, and follow him all the way.

Salvation Given

For this commandment which I command you this day is not too hard, neither is it far off for you.

—Deuteronomy 30:11

Remember, he gave us Ten Commandments, not suggestions. How's that for obvious?

Are you feeling lucky?

> Although I told you, you would not listen. You rebelled against
> the command of the Lord and presumptuously went off into the
> hill country.
> —DEUTERONOMY 1:43, NRSV

When is the last time you went to the gas station?

Solution Offered

Are you one of those people who like to frolic in the fuel-light warning
world? I'm convinced that there are three kinds of people driving today:

The person who stops at a gas station as soon as the fuel light comes
on.

The person who always drives a car on empty...until the very last
fumes run out as he or she pulls into the station.

The person whose fuel gauge is always broken and just goes on faith.

Regardless of which one you are (or if you take the bus or ride a
bike), you probably at least know someone who fits into one of these
categories.

You might think that I'm going to say that we need to be like the
third person and just drive around on faith, as far as the Lord will take
us...but you'd be wrong. Yes, we need to trust in God and rely on him.
The above verse, however, cautions us that God gives us those fuel-light
warnings for a reason. Driving around on faith with blind luck and no
plan might get you here and there, but sooner or later you'll get burned
and find yourself stuck in the middle of nowhere.

Take this verse from Deuteronomy in a modern context; it is speaking
to the second and third type of person in the list above. God warns
us when our spiritual tanks are getting too low, when we're tempting

fate, and when we're coasting to a dead end. Most mechanics will tell you that a good rule of thumb is to never let your tank get below a quarter full. It keeps your engine running smoothly. When it gets below a quarter tank, the engine has to work a lot harder, and it wears on your car.

Most priests and spiritual mentors will tell you the same thing about your faith tank. Jesus taught the apostles the importance of keeping their tanks filled. You've heard that you can't give what we don't have, and as a Christian who is trying to live your faith in this world today, you have a responsibility to Christ to heed that fuel light. When it comes on (from overwork or lack of prayer or, worse yet, sin), pull your car into the station of the Church and fill up on the sacraments. In fact, we should be topping off our tanks every day on prayer and Scripture, because you never know when someone you care about will be out of gas and might need to siphon some of ours. Even those in electric cars need the power of the Spirit, and the Church is the premiere power outlet.

Those of us who know where the gas (or power) is found need to be thinking ahead for those that don't.

Salvation Given

> Although I told you, you would not listen. You rebelled against the command of the Lord and presumptuously went off into the hill country.
> —DEUTERONOMY 1:43, NRSV

Prayer turns a regular unleaded life into a premium one. Without God, you're not going anywhere.

A man was there named Zacchaeus; he was a chief tax collector and was rich. He was trying to see who Jesus was, but on account of the crowd he could not, because he was short in stature. So he ran ahead and climbed a sycamore tree to see him, because he was going to pass that way. When Jesus came to the place, he looked up and said to him, "Zacchaeus, hurry and come down; for I must stay at your house today."

—Luke 19:2–5, NRSV

When is the last time you climbed a tree?

The older you get, the more you may need to…

Solution Offered

You may be familiar with this story already, but I'd encourage you to read it again in its entirety (see Luke 19:1–10). The story is a simple one, but, as usual, God is teaching us something quite profound.

Here we have Zacchaeus, a short, wealthy, curious little guy who was despised by all. Now, before anyone thinks I'm being too harsh, let me explain. We know that he was wealthy and short because St. Luke tells us that directly (19:2–3). We know he was despised because he was the chief tax collector (they weren't a real popular bunch) in Jericho. We know he was curious because of the above passage, where, because of his short stature, we're told that he was forced to climb a tree to get a glimpse of this Jesus guy that everyone had been talking about.

Little did Zack (for short) know as he scaled the bark of that syca-more tree just how drastically his life was about to change—for the better. Once on the limb, he stared into the merciful eyes of Christ. He heard Jesus's voice calling him, not only out of the tree, but out of his selfishness, pride, and money-driven way of life. That night, Zack sat in Jesus's presence while the Lord sat at the sinner's table. Once Zacchaeus broke bread with the Lord, God broke his heart for anything else. Once you've tasted heaven, earth is pretty bland in comparison. What good would all his money be without God in his life?

After that brief encounter with Jesus, Zacchaeus's life was forever changed. It is impossible to imagine, after an afternoon and evening like he had, how differently he viewed himself. Other people spoke about Zacchaeus differently now, too. People looked at him differently. After his personal encounter with Christ—in the flesh—he was transformed.

These kinds of biblical stories were a difficult concept for me for a long time, because that's all they were—stories. I had gone to church every Sunday. I knew the characters and the plot. I knew the prayers. I had gone to Catholic school; I knew the rules. I was properly formed in Catholic Christianity, but I was not yet transformed by Christ. I knew about Christ, but I had not had a deep, personal encounter with him (or so I thought). I knew "who he was," but I didn't know him. I was afraid to climb the tree.

It was not until I surrendered a little bit, not until I went out on a limb, that I really began to encounter the real Jesus Christ. The more I admitted that I didn't have it all together, the more real he became to me. The more desire I expressed in getting to know the real Jesus, the more I wanted to get to know him. The more I still want to know him. It is after that transformation happened that the unbending truth and unyielding power contained in the formation really begin to take root and bear fruit.

Never underestimate how quickly your life can be forever changed once you have seen Jesus's face up close. Stare into his eyes of mercy in the sacrament of confession—it's called reconciliation for a reason. Hear his voice in the sacred Scriptures calling you out of yourself, your comfort zone, and your culture. Sit in his presence in Adoration. Share the meal with Christ that will last forever in the Eucharist.

Let's learn from Zacchaeus's passion and urgency. Never doubt how immediately God can work in your life when you show that kind of desire to see him up close and personal. Don't wait until you find yourself up a tree. If you have a desire to get to know God more deeply today, then tell him that in your prayer.

Salvation Given

A man was there named Zacchaeus; he was a chief tax collector and was rich. He was trying to see who Jesus was, but on account of the crowd he could not, because he was short in stature. So he ran ahead and climbed a sycamore tree to see him, because he was going to pass that way. When Jesus came to the place, he looked up and said to him, "Zacchaeus, hurry and come down; for I must stay at your house today."

—LUKE 19:2–5, NRSV

You are never too old (or young) to climb that tree for God...after all, he climbed a tree for you on Good Friday.

The first thing I need; the last thing I want.

But many that are first will be last, and the last first.
—MATTHEW 19:30

When does your patience get tested the most? I know when mine does. Do you love waiting in line as much as I do?

Solution Offered

I'm serious. There are few things we do during the course of the week that exercise our Christianity and make us use our Christian virtue of patience the way waiting in line does. We are a culture of people who don't like to wait. We like to have everything now.

Let me give you a few examples of what I mean. See how many you can relate to:

Sitting in the left-hand turn lane, the light changes to a green arrow, but the driver in front sits in the car, not moving, not paying attention. Choice: Be patient or lay on the horn until the person goes deaf.

Standing in the express lane at the grocery when the person in front of you wants to use coupons and pay with an out-of-state check. Choice: Be patient or roll your eyes so far back that you could go blind.

Waiting to buy a bottle of water at a convenience store, the person in front of you has thirty-two separate items and needs to buy lottery tickets right then. Choice: Be patient or sigh so loudly that your exhales sound like a hurricane moving through the store.

Waiting at the counter to order food at a restaurant, the counter employee talks to the person who calls in an order, who didn't take the time to drive there like I did. Choice: Be patient or make an unnecessary comment.

Well, you get the point.

I'm not saying it's always easy.

I'm not saying that sometimes it can't eat away at your last nerve.

I'm not even saying that sometimes situations don't necessitate action.

But that's what being a Christian in today's world is all about. It's not always easy, people can get on your last nerve, and some situations require action but not all.

Was Jesus speaking specifically about lines when he uttered this verse? No, not exactly. Would Jesus be a model of patience and restraint on a daily basis? You had better believe it.

If God has that kind of patience, couldn't you and I each be a little more patient in the heat of summer, when everyone's a little worn out? Or in the winter, when the sky is gray for days, the wind bites, and snow clogs the roads?

I'll try if you will. Start with today, and take it one day at a time.

Salvation Given

But many that are first will be last, and the last first.
—Matthew 19:30

You need lessons? Call my mom. She's got more patience than a hospital.

For God is not so unjust as to overlook your work and the love
which you showed for his sake in serving the saints, as you still do.
—HEBREWS 6:10

Do you ever get sick of acting like a Christian? Do you ever wish that
you could pretend that you didn't know better and do whatever you
wanted? Do you ever wonder if God sees all that you do for him or
sacrifice for him? Do you ever worry that he forgets or doesn't notice?

Solution Offered

In your opinion, is it more difficult to be a Catholic Christian when
someone is persecuting you or when someone who isn't very Christian
is getting ahead or having an easier time than you are?

Speaking personally, I can deal with people who make fun of me
for going to church, or reading the Bible, or praying before a meal in
a restaurant. I can even deal with people telling me that "Catholics
aren't going to heaven" or that I "worship Mary and statues." That
stuff doesn't bother me nearly as much as when the kid who cheats gets
an A and I study and get a B or when the kid who shoplifts has nicer
clothes than I do or when the guy next door cheats on his taxes and
drives a nicer car than mine or when I remain patient in traffic while
the rude person next to me cuts in front.

Sometimes I want to scream, or I want to get the guy next to me by
the neck and just—

But then it hits me: Is that what Jesus is calling me to do?

It is really hard to be a Catholic Christian in today's society and live
the way that we are called to live. No one is denying that.

I used to look up into the sky on bad days and say, "Hey, God, what are you thinking?" "Why me, God, and why today?" "I go to church, I try to follow you, and yet you're putting this in front of me to deal with? What did I do to you?"

Then it hits me even harder. God is not some evil, vindictive ruler trying to make my life miserable. Every trial that gets set before me is an invitation and an opportunity: an invitation to call on God and an opportunity to respond in faithfulness and depend on him.

If you have those moments when you feel as though no one notices the sacrifices that you go through because of your faith, don't worry anymore. Make this verse your battle cry. Someone does notice, and that Someone is Jesus. God knows what we do and, even more, what we don't do. You and I will be rewarded when our time comes. The trick is to trust that God sees all and remembers all.

Salvation Given

For God is not so unjust as to overlook your work and the love which you showed for his sake in serving the saints, as you still do.
—HEBREWS 6:10

Our salvation may have cost us nothing, but true discipleship will cost us everything.

The children of God and the children of the devil are revealed in this way: all who do not do what is right are not from God, nor are those who do not love their brothers and sisters.

—1 JOHN 3:10, NRSV

Can love and hate coexist?

My mother had a rule when I was little: I could get away with saying that I hated lima beans or that I hated doing my chores, but never, under any circumstances, was I allowed to say that I hated another person. It didn't matter who it was, even the school bully; if I said "I hate (fill in person here)," my mom immediately stopped and corrected me.

"It's all right to dislike someone—even to dislike them a lot—but you don't ever hate someone. Never, ever let your heart be filled with hate for another soul. It will hurt you far more than the other person in the long run," she would explain.

Please, take a second and reread the above verse from St. John. My mom was right—she was even paraphrasing Scripture without knowing it. (Mom, if you're reading this, way to go).

In the past several months, there have been plenty of news stories to demonstrate how much evil and hatred exist in the world. I think I've felt just about every emotion imaginable, as I am sure many of you have, too. Spend ten minutes online, and you'll encounter something outside of God's hopes and design for us. Our screens are filled at every turn with ugliness, it seems. Our screens are also filled with beauty if we look closely enough and in the right places. On the average day, scrolling through my own feed, I'm overwhelmed by others' posts. I feel everything from disbelief, compassion, grief, uneasiness, concern, wonder, hope, and even deep anger rush through my body on any given week. I even feel hatred sometimes. Not hatred for my fellow man, but hatred for the acts and actions of some of them, and for the evil and darkness and hatred that must exist within their hearts and minds.

Yet, even with dark realities staring us in the face—atrocities that occur because of race, religion, or political belief, we as Christians are called to think bigger and love more deeply. We are called to look at everything done in the name of justice or revenge and view it through the eyes and heart of Jesus Christ.

Being a true Catholic means to love justice and respect life in all its forms and stages.

We can best honor God by respecting all others—beyond religious beliefs, political differences, or nationalities—and by finding what we have in common with them, as we do with our brothers and sisters of other Christian denominations. We must constantly strive to focus on the fact that we are all made in the image and likeness of God (see Genesis 1:26–27).

The passage from 1 John reminds us that you and I are the children of God when we act in righteousness and love our brother. It's that simple.

It's OK to be upset and even angry over things that happen around the world or show up in your social media feed, but don't let them steal your joy, cause you to sin, or destroy your hope. Put any energy that is tempted to hate into loving others instead.

If that doesn't work, maybe we'll have my mom give them a call. And if my earthly mom is too busy, we can always call on our heavenly mother, Mary, to intercede (pray on their behalf) for them. Sooner or later, even the hardest and darkest hearts crumble when they are placed in her hands.

Salvation Given

> The children of God and the children of the devil are revealed in this way: all who do not do what is right are not from God, nor are those who do not love their brothers and sisters.
> —1 JOHN 3:10, NRSV

When you are personally in pain, it's always harder to love someone than to hate them, but Christ did it…even when hanging on the cross (see Luke 23:34). Ask Jesus to help you in those areas where you feel helpless to love.

But now the Lord my God has given me rest on every side; there is neither adversary nor misfortune.

—1 KINGS 5:4

Were you ever afraid of the dark as a kid?

Solution Offered

People suffer from different fears: fear of commitment, fear of loneliness, fear of poverty, fear of death. One fairly consistent fear for many, beginning in childhood and extending into adult life, is the "fear of the unknown."

What will happen with "this situation"?

What will happen with "this relationship"? What will happen with "this job"?

What will happen with my family, my future, my...?

When I was a child, provided for and protected by my parents, fear wasn't very common. At night, though, when I was in bed and my room was dark, with no one around, that's when I'd get scared. It was in that moment, too, that even normal household noises would all sound like approaching death.

Why? Because in that world of darkness existed the unknown. I couldn't see clearly, my feet weren't on the ground, and I was vulnerable. Somehow, though, after I prayed, I would fall asleep. It was as though my guardian angel was protecting me.

It's like that in life sometimes, too. The unknown can get a little scary, and being vulnerable to others or to God is not a popular concept.

Why, when the unknown confronts or scares us, do we not follow the lessons we learned as children? Why do we try, so often, to figure everything out or take control, rather than trusting in the fact that God is watching over us?

Jesus is the light, the night light in the sometimes scary bedroom we call the world around us.

Are there any fears of the unknown in your life right now?

Well, handle it like a six-year-old: Say a prayer, roll over, and rest in the promise that God, the ultimate parent, is with his child. He is watching over you, protecting you, and guiding you safely through the darkness to the light of a new day.

Salvation Given

But now the Lord my God has given me rest on every side; there is neither adversary nor misfortune.

—1 KINGS 5:4

I pray the Lord my soul to keep. How about you?

God's no quitter.

I have great confidence in you; I have great pride in you; I am
filled with comfort. With all our affliction, I am overjoyed.

—2 CORINTHIANS 7:4

How often does someone compliment or affirm you? Do you have a lot
of those days when you feel as though everyone's against you? Do you
ever sit and wonder, "Are you there, God? Are you still with me?"

Solution Offered

He's always as close as an invitation, a prayer.

The people in Corinth were in bad shape: pretty self-involved, pretty
worldly, and not the most disciplined Christians. Yet, despite their faults
and sinfulness, St. Paul (like Jesus) didn't give up on them. He encouraged them.

That's kind of the way it is with us, huh? You and I both know that
we're sinners, that we're not perfect. Yet he never gives up on us. Why?
No, seriously, do you ever think about the reason why he doesn't give
up on us?

Like St. Paul, God has confidence and pride in us. He is filled with
encouragement and overflowing with joy.

But why? Well, that's where it gets tricky in this verse, so pay attention, folks.

The verse for today says that Paul is "overjoyed" over "our affliction." Am I trying to tell you that God takes joy in your trials, in the
things that cause you anger, that cause you worry, even that cause you
to question him?

No. Rather, what St. Paul's telling us is that because we have afflictions (trials) in our life, we know that God is at work in our lives. We

should rejoice in our afflictions because they are a sign that we're maturing in our faith, that God knows we can handle them.

So when you face trials or difficulties, don't curse God for them. Thank God for them.

In 1 Corinthians we're told that God will never tempt us beyond what we can handle. We should have confidence that God won't abandon us when things get difficult; in fact, when things get difficult, God is that much closer.

Just like St. Paul, I gotta say that I, an insignificant little Bible Geek, have great confidence and pride in you. I am thankful that you've taken the time to read this book and hopefully apply even more of God's challenging truths to your life. If I'm this excited that you care about the Word of God (the most glorious of all words ever spoken in the history of creation), just think how joyful Jesus must be today.

If you have a lot of hurdles in your life today, say, "Thank you, God, for believing in me and for creating me smarter and stronger than I might want to believe."

Salvation Given

I have great confidence in you; I have great pride in you; I am filled with comfort. With all our affliction, I am overjoyed.
—2 CORINTHIANS 7:4

I've had a really tough week. God must really love me, huh?

WALKING
THE
WALK

Catholic
Christianity
is not for
wimps

Jesus "crossed" me, and I'm glad.

> Therefore I intend always to remind you of these things, though
> you know them and are established in the truth that you have.
> —2 PETER 1:12

What does the word cross mean to you?

I don't mean the cross of Christ; I mean the word cross.

It's actually used pretty frequently in language today, but not always about Jesus. Whenever I hear the word, though, I think of Jesus. Stick with me here.

Solution Offered

The cross is a sign of pain, of awareness, and of sacrifice.

The cross is a sign of promise, of hope, and of safety.

The cross is a sign of wisdom, of truth, and of victory.

And in the past two thousand years, nothing has changed. It's still a sign of all of those things—in many ways.

You see, if you

cross your eyes, you'll be in pain;

stop at the railroad crossing, you show awareness of the dangers around you;

cross something off your Christmas wish list, you're making a sacrifice;

cross your heart, you're making a promise;

cross your fingers, you're showing hope;

cross in the crosswalk, you're striving for safety;

do the crossword, you grow in wisdom;

cross-examine a witness, you get closer to discovering the truth;

cross the finish line first, you get the victory.

The word *cross* has incredible meaning in our everyday lives. Pay close attention to the words people are saying, and ask yourself how many of them lead you to contemplate Christ and his immense love for you. God can use anything—and anyone—to get our attention each day and turn our hearts back to him.

The verse from St. Peter reminds us that God is doing just that—reminding us, constantly, that he is very much alive and very much at work for our salvation. We need only to become more aware of it daily.

Take a step in faith. Trust in him. He will not let you down.

Salvation Given

Therefore I intend always to remind you of these things, though you know them and are established in the truth that you have.
—2 PETER 1:12

He wants your path and his path to cross daily.

> For we are his workmanship, created in Christ Jesus for good
> works, which God prepared beforehand, that we should walk in
> them.
>
> —EPHESIANS 2:10

Did you know that God wants only one thing from you and me? It's not
to be the smartest, or the strongest, or the prettiest, or the wisest. What
does God want us to be more than anything? Give up? All right, since
we're friends I'll tell you.

Solution Offered

What God wants from us, more than anything else in the world, is for
us to be holy.

Now, what does that word mean to you? To a lot of people, *holy*
means quiet or solemn. Other people think *holy* means that you spend
24/7 on your knees in prayer. That's not exactly what God is calling
us to do. We know this from what St. Paul shares here with the folks in
Ephesus.

Read the verse again. He calls us (you and me) God's "workmanship,
created in Christ Jesus." That means that we were created, formed, and
molded by God for a purpose.

Paul also says that the reason we were created was "for good works,
which God prepared beforehand." That means that before you were
even born, God had a plan for you, and that plan was for you to be holy
and active in things that glorify him and build his kingdom. Remember,
Paul says "for good works." Do you remember what I said in the intro-
duction to this book about fish and birds?

Fish swim, birds fly. Fish and birds give glory to God by doing what they were designed to do. In the same way, we humans give glory to God by doing what we are designed to do. We do not give glory to God by lying, stealing, getting drunk, or abusing our sexuality. We give glory to God by living lives worthy of the call that we've received. We give glory to God by living our lives according to a different standard, a standard of sacrifice and service, the standard of Jesus Christ.

The best thing about the call to holiness is that you never have to wonder what to do in a situation to please God; you just do what Jesus would do.

Salvation Given

For we are his workmanship, created in Christ Jesus for good works, which God prepared beforehand, that we should walk in them.

—Ephesians 2:10

The greatest contribution anyone can make is the example of a holy life.

—Anonymous

> Blessed are you when people revile you and persecute you and
> utter all kinds of evil against you falsely on my account.
> —MATTHEW 5:11

Does it sometimes feel like people are always on your case? Do you
have anyone in your life who is consistently mean or rude to you? How
about when it comes to your faith? Are you ever attacked for it?

Solution Offered

If you answered yes to any of the questions above, you're in good shape.
Scratch that...you're not just in good shape; you're in great shape.

You're in great shape, that is, if you are looking at everything in the
right way.

Jesus's most famous sermon (the Sermon on the Mount) gave us the
Lord's prayer and taught us about everything from heaven and hell to
marriage and divorce, and even God's wisdom on dealing with stress.
His sermon begins, however, with the famous Beatitudes.

Some of you reading this have heard (or read) the Beatitudes a
thousand times—you may even be able to repeat them from memory.
Others of you may be hearing about these for the first time. In either
case, I want you to read the next few lines from Matthew 5:1–11 and
think about who is said to be blessed in Jesus's eyes...

Blessed are the poor in spirit...

Blessed are they who mourn...

Blessed are the meek...

Blessed are they who hunger and thirst for righteousness...

Blessed are the merciful...

Blessed are the clean of heart...

Blessed are the peacemakers...

Blessed are they who are persecuted for the sake of righteousness...

At first glance, these are all counterintuitive, meaning that they seem to go against what we'd call "logical." The more we pray through them, though, we see that Christ gives us these beatitudes because he wants these to *be* our *attitudes*.

What attitude do we hear and find in these beatitudes? We discover God's attitude.

When I read the Beatitudes, I realize that I need an attitude adjustment most days. Too often during the course of the week, my attitude is not what I read here and not what a Christian attitude ought to be toward others. Read through, again, which groups of people are truly "blessed" in God's eyes...it's not the proud, the powerful, the snobby, the cruel, the violent, or the self-centered.

There are going to "be attitudes" around us that we don't like—that's just a fact, and we cannot control that. The only person's attitude and actions you can control are your own.

The key is to keep this passage in mind at all times, especially when you don't feel like it.

Remember, if Christianity were easy, everyone would be living it.

Salvation Given

Blessed are you when people revile you and persecute you and utter all kinds of evil against you falsely on my account.
—MATTHEW 5:11

Christ, help my attitude to be your attitude.

I'm scared of clowns, but Christ isn't.

God chose what is foolish in the world to shame the wise, God
chose what is weak in the world to shame the strong.

—1 Corinthians 1:27

Have you ever been told to grow up? Do you ever just act a little
foolishly?

Solution Offered

I was driving the other day with one of my favorite bands blaring on
my stereo. It was a sunny afternoon, the top was off my Jeep, and I was
singing at the top of my lungs to the music (even when I was sitting at
the stoplight). When it hit me that I was singing (very loudly) with the
top off, I looked at the cars next to me. People were smiling, sort of
laughing, and my first instinct was to be a little embarrassed. But then
I got to thinking.

Who cares if I look like a dork? God sure doesn't. And I need to
remember that.

For a long time, I was really concerned with what people thought
about me. Maybe you've even felt this way before. Maybe you still do
sometimes.

As I grow in my faith, though, it becomes clearer and clearer to me
that I'm not out to impress anyone, or please anyone, except God.
Because if I'm really living for him, everything else and every other
relationship falls into place.

So that's why I'm the Bible Geek and a Jesus freak and any other
name that gets thrown out there. And I'm proud to be, too. Let the
world call me foolish or weak or any other demeaning adjective it can

think of, because God can do amazing things with the weak and the outcast. Just read the Gospels.

What's foolish in the eyes of the world isn't foolish at all in God's eyes. He's more interested in the state of my heart and my soul than in whether or not I fit in with what is considered cool or normal.

I wanna be a fool, all right, a fool for Christ. What's sad is that many think that living for Christ is so foolish. Nothing could be further from the truth. When someone sees you've gotten into your faith, for instance, and they (negatively) mutter, "You've changed," you might be tempted to take it as an insult. Why? It's actually one of the greatest compliments someone can offer you on your journey of faith. The fact is that you're not only thinking about changing but are actually putting the thoughts and impulses into practice? Well done! In fact, if you're really following Christ, you'll always be changing...and growing and improving.

Salvation Given

God chose what is foolish in the world to shame the wise, God chose what is weak in the world to shame the strong.
—1 CORINTHIANS 1:27

I'm with Christ. I'd be a fool not to be.

The Book is always better than the movie.

And now, Lord…help your servants to proclaim your message with all boldness.

—Acts 4:29, JB

Seen any good movies lately? Experienced God lately?

Solution Offered

It never ceases to amaze me. I can be in a coffee shop, in a grocery store, at work, even waiting to tell the guy at the fast food place what condiments I want, and somehow I (or the person I'm with) starts talking about movies.

"Have you seen any good movies lately?" someone asks.

"I just saw the best (or worst) movie last night," someone offers.

Why is it that it's so common to talk about movies but not about God in everyday conversation? Why do we spend so much time recommending movies to watch but so little time recommending that our friends and family read the Bible or check out church?

Why is it that some days I spend more time searching Netflix or iTunes for new releases than I do praying? How much more time do I spend on Twitter or Instagram than actually listening to God? Sad, but true.

It's not always comfortable to have conversations about God. It's not always comfortable to bring God into the work or school environment.

Why is that?

Maybe there's a comfort in "just recommending" a movie and not God. My friends don't have to watch the movie. It's their choice.

It's the same way with God, though. Will people download (pray) or watch (spend time with him) based on our advice? Some will; some won't. All we can do is recommend the best title:

Jesus, the Lord, our Savior.

Maybe it's time I step back and consider the topics I discuss the most. It's time to take a look at me.

Am I ever ashamed to talk about God?

Do I ever not bring God up because I'm afraid it might make people uncomfortable?

What am I called to do? What am I called today to be?

Next time movie rentals or new releases come up in your conversation, think about him. The person you're talking to might really benefit from a couple minutes of the greatest story ever told.

Salvation Given

And now, Lord,…help your servants to proclaim your message with all boldness.

—Acts 4:29, JB

God is the most important person in your life. He is the best gift you have to give another. Do you agree with those two statements? Now, what are you going to do about it?

Jesus doesn't water ski.

The purpose in a man's mind is like deep water, but a man of understanding will draw it out.

—Proverbs 20:5

In your opinion, are you a deep person? Do you think that your friends would consider you a person of great depth? How about your family? Why does it matter? Good questions.

Solution Offered

When I was a kid we used to go to the lake and the ocean a lot. We'd go boating, we'd water-ski, and sometimes we'd just anchor the boat and swim around or float atop the water for hours. I really enjoyed spending that time on the water.

As I grew older and (hopefully) a little more mature, however, my appreciation for the water really began to change. Going snorkeling and scuba diving the first time really opened my eyes. There was an entire world that existed beneath the surface I used to swim and ski across—a world of life, color, beauty, and depth.

Then it hit me. Most of my relationships at the time, especially my relationship with God, were surface relationships with no real depth. My relationship with my girlfriend, with many of my friends, with members of my family: all surface, lacking depth.

Maybe I was afraid to open myself up. Maybe I knew that if I did go deeper in my faith, my life would get more difficult, or I couldn't have fun anymore.

God designed us and created us to experience a depth and a love that would make some people shout with joy but make most people wet their pants. Many people are afraid to go deep. Letting down our guard, showing vulnerability, forgiving others, affirming one another, living for God and not ourselves: This is the "purpose in a man's mind" that the "understanding" child of God "draws out," as this verse points out.

God formed your heart, and the Holy Spirit that dwells there is not a surface type spirit. The Spirit is one of fire, passion, courage, wisdom, and love. Tap into it.

This weekend, take off the skis, put on the flippers, and go deeper than normal. Tell someone how he or she has made a difference in your life. Speak to those around you as if it's the last time you'll see them. Take thirty seconds to affirm someone who needs it. That's the depth your heart was created for, relishes in, and is designed to share.

Salvation Given

The purpose in a man's mind is like deep water, but a man of understanding will draw it out.

—PROVERBS 20:5

On the surface I'm just a geek. It's the Bible that provides the depth.

I dare you to try this.

The apostles said to the Lord, "Increase our faith!"
—LUKE 17:5

What or whom do you pray for the most? If you look at the time you spend in prayer, how much is spent on you, on others, on stuff you want or need, and so on? Most people say that they pray but add that they should pray more. That makes me wonder, "When we do pray, what are we praying for?"

Solution Offered

We need to be more like the apostles. I don't mean we should wear sandals everywhere (imagine those things in the snow), and I don't mean that we should spend more time fishing (that won't pay the bills). Today we just see the apostles being so simple and so straightforward with Jesus. Speaking for myself, I can learn a lot from them. I always seem to make my relationship with Jesus more complicated than it needs to be.

How about you? You feel like taking a risk today? You want a life of adventure? You want to live on the edge? You want danger?

If you don't, then stop reading.

Now for those of you who do: You can juggle knives, walk over hot coals, skydive without a parachute, leave Mass early (that's very dangerous), swim right after eating, run with scissors, play fetch with a tiger. Guys, you can even tell your girlfriend that you don't like her outfit. But if you really, really want to live dangerously, if you want to live on the edge, pray. Nothing in this world is as dangerous as prayer.

Why is prayer so dangerous? Simple, because our prayers can be answered. Lives can change, souls can be saved, and peace can be found—all through prayer. If we could pray for only one thing a day, today's request from the apostles would be a great prayer. "Increase our faith," they beg. Imagine if you and I had more faith in God—more faith in his plan (see Romans 9), in his timetable (see Ecclesiastes 3), in our future (see Ephesians 2), in his perfect love (see John 15).

You want to live dangerously today? Repeat after me: "Lord, please go to work in my life and use the talents you've given me to glorify you. Lord, I beg you to increase my faith and my desire to read your Word. I give you permission to turn my world upside down. Send your Spirit to overwhelm my stubbornness and laziness and teach me how to really pray."

Salvation Given

The apostles said to the Lord, "Increase our faith!"
—LUKE 17:5

Catholicism is not a spectator sport. Get in the game today.

[Look] to Jesus, the pioneer and perfecter of our faith, who for the joy that was set before him endured the cross, despising the shame, and is seated at the right hand of the throne of God.

—HEBREWS 12:2

Have you ever wanted to be a superhero?

Solution Offered

During the summer I often think back to when I was a child, playing with friends until the very last glimmer of sunlight had disappeared from the evening sky and the bugs came out in full force. My favorite game (when I was about five or six) was when we'd each pick different superheroes to be, and we'd defend the neighborhood from the tyranny of the bad guys who lived in the dark (actually, vacant) house at the end of the street.

What amazes me now is how a simple bed sheet could transform me into an invincible superhero. That's all it took, a bed sheet tied around my neck. Once that sheet was tied, my arms went straight out in front of me, and I made a sort of swooshing sound and ran in circles—I mean, uh, flew in circles—until I landed (making fists with my hands, resting them upon my waist, and then posing for a few seconds). Can anyone relate?

Well, a couple weeks back I was getting ready to go into a not-so-nice area of town to do a talk at a church. I hadn't been wearing my cross a lot lately (it's too hot in the summertime), but that night I grabbed it and put it on. It caught my attention in the mirror for some reason, and I pulled it off and looked at it.

I realized, at that moment, that what I was feeling I hadn't felt since I was a kid playing Superman. I felt absolutely invincible again. I had been to confession and Mass that day. I had spent some great time in prayer and learned some amazing new things in the Scriptures. At that point I was invincible, and that cross signified everything I wanted to stand for and everything I would give my life to defend.

For centuries after Jesus's death, the cross was seen as a symbol of defeat, of shame. It wasn't until the fourth century that the cross was seen widely as a true symbol of victory and Christian pride.

Since that night, every day when I put on my cross, I take a few seconds, look at it in the mirror, and thank God for the greatest super-hero ever, Jesus, the conqueror of evil and death. I also thank him for the opportunity to follow in his steps, helping to defend my own little community from the bad guys.

Superman got his power from the sun. What a coincidence. I get my power from the Son, too. And so do you.

Salvation Given

[Look] to Jesus, the pioneer and perfecter of our faith, who for the joy that was set before him endured the cross, despising the shame, and is seated at the right hand of the throne of God.
—HEBREWS 12:2

One difference between Christ and Superman: Jesus doesn't want his identity to remain a secret. Don't be afraid to tell everyone.

He's usually right where you left him.

> I will get up and go to my father, and I will say to him, "Father,
> I have sinned against heaven and before you; I am no longer
> worthy to be called your son; treat me like one of your hired
> hands." So he set off and went to his father. But while he was still
> far off, his father saw him and was filled with compassion; he ran
> and put his arms around him and kissed him.
> —LUKE 15:18–20

Do you ever feel as though areas of your life are a mess? Ever feel like
you can't feel God's presence, almost like he is nowhere to be found?

You're not alone.

Solution Offered

This verse above from St. Luke comes to us from the famous parable
of the Prodigal Son in chapter 15. You've probably heard the story
hundreds of times, as I have, but often we miss some of the most important details in the stories we've heard the most frequently.

Because of the popularity of this parable, for centuries people have
believed the term *prodigal* to be a good thing. Well, it is—and it isn't.
The word *prodigal* actually means "recklessly wasteful," as in the case of
this son who had foolishly spent his entire inheritance on the temporary
and the worldly. The word *prodigal* also means "extremely generous,"
however, as in the case of the father, who was amazingly generous with
his mercy, compassion, and fortune to his returning son. One of the
most impressive parts of this story is contained in verse 20. The passage
reads, "He [the father] ran to his son…"

Now, keep in mind that the son had asked for his inheritance before
the father was even dead (a huge slap in the face and a sign of disrespect

in the ancient world). Not only had he then spent all the money, he had wasted it. It had gotten so bad for the son, in fact, that he was literally lying in the mud fighting the pigs for their food. And now, looking at the mess his life had become—professionally, socially, and literally (he was covered in mud and smelled like a pig)—he decided to return to his father and beg his forgiveness.

Here is where the story goes from being one of the prodigal son who wasted his undeserved blessings to the prodigal father who seems to waste (in the eyes of the older brother) all kinds of mercy and forgiveness upon a child who had deserted him. Notice, though, that it is not a waste—not in the eyes of the father.

Upon seeing his son returning, the father could have sat in the house, waiting for the son, making him sweat, refusing to forgive him, or even making him grovel at his feet or work as a slave. Instead, the father not only forgave him, he ran to meet him. When they were face-to-face, the father did not condemn his child for the mess he had made of his life or shun him for his muddy filth or swine-like smell. No, the father embraced the returning, repentant son. Why, you ask? Because that is what good parents do: They love, even when their children haven't acted in such a way as to deserve it.

In a similar way, even when I make a mess of my life—through selfishness, poor decisions, or apathy—God is not only waiting to embrace me in my mess, but he is actually pursuing me; he is running to me. We aren't just seeking God—God the Father is constantly seeking us! Even if I feel as though I'm too messy or that he is wasting his time or mercy on me, he loves me all the more, and he loves me prodigally, with extreme and unlimited generosity.

This week, don't focus on the small messes of life or on where you've been. Instead, look toward God, your loving Father, and allow him not only to approach you, but to embrace you in your messiness. The child ran back to the father…you do the same.

_____ *Salvation Given*

I will get up and go to my father, and I will say to him, "Father, I have sinned against heaven and before you; I am no longer worthy to be called your son; treat me like one of your hired hands." So he set off and went to his father. But while he was still far off, his father saw him and was filled with compassion; he ran and put his arms around him and kissed him.

—Luke 15:18–20

As we see here, it is never a waste running to God; it's a waste of time not to do so.

There are no beds in heaven.

And on the seventh day God finished the work that he had done,
and he rested on the seventh day from all the work that he had
done. So God blessed the seventh day and hallowed it...
—Genesis 2:2–3

What are you doing on Sunday? Yes, this is a trick question.

Solution Offered

When I was a kid, the weekends were so relaxing. Sleeping in, watching
cartoons, playing outside—there was nothing better. As I grew older,
however, weekends changed. In middle school and high school, weekends were taken up with games and work and service projects, trips and
retreats, and even multiple jobs. Eventually I became a husband and
father, and now weekends are often synonymous with getting caught
up on laundry, paying bills, grocery shopping, working out, washing the
car, cleaning the house...the list goes on and on.

Too bad the laundry list of activities always seems to happen when I
have time off. How about you? Do you find yourself way too busy most
of the time? Do you ever get stressed or overwhelmed trying to balance
family obligations, relationships, work, school, sports, and other activities? There never seems to be enough hours in the day or lack of activities to occupy our time. So God gave us the weekends to get caught
up, right? Wrong. That's the trap, and God wants us to be forewarned,
which is why the Spirit inspired the author of Genesis to write it down
for us in the Bible.

For most people—Christians included—Sundays have become catch-
up days. We use Sundays to get all kinds of other stuff done—housework,

yard work, homework, and so on—rather than using it for the purpose it was designed for: rest.

I love this passage from Genesis specifically because it is so simple. It says God rested. Oftentimes we (being as busy as we are) read that as, "Well, God must have been tired after creating light, water, the universe, the planets and stars and earth, and mountains and valleys and animals and humans, and everything...so he deserved a rest." That interpretation reveals our humanity and our overly busy shortsightedness.

Was God really tired? Is that what Genesis was trying to get across to us? No, not at all. God doesn't get tired—he's God. If he got tired, he wouldn't be divine; he'd be human. Instead, this little moment in Genesis exists to show us that we need to rest. God is modeling behavior for us, the same way he did when Jesus was baptized in the River Jordan (it's not like Jesus needed baptism—he was sinless (again, he's God). He gives us this example of rest and then gives us the command to "keep holy the Sabbath" because he understood that, in our humanity, we'd take on too much and rest too little. We are better at being human *doings* than human *beings.* Remember what we learned from Martha and Mary? (See Luke 10:38–42.)

That isn't to say we should only sleep (this is for any of you who live for your beds and are getting overly excited by this entry right now). God doesn't want you to be a sloth, either. God gave us rest so we could work, not work so we could rest. At the same time, God gave us the gift of rest and the gift of the Sabbath (Sunday) to ensure that we were spending time with one another and with him, not just catching up on other things.

"That's all fine and good, BG (Big Guy)," you might say. "But when am I supposed to get all this stuff done, anyway?" That's a fair question. How about a fair answer? Is God necessarily calling you to take on as much as you have? Our first answer is always yes, and maybe that's true, but sometimes we need to take an honest step back and reevaluate over time. Often we take on more than we should, commit to more than is healthy, and attempt more than is sane, in the name of getting things done. Here is one of the most basic lessons in moral development: Just because we can do something, doesn't mean we ought to do it.

The seventh day—every Sabbath day—serves as a reminder to us that God wants to be primary in our lives. God wants to spend time with us, not just between errands or chores but when we are at our best, when our attention is undivided. Put simply, in essence every Sunday is a holy day (holiday), an entire day set aside to break from the work, the stress, and the schedules, to enter into our family's lives and into the life of God.

How much happier so many families would be if we actually did break and just spend time together as we are commanded by God to do. Just a pipe dream, you might think? Not in the families I've seen. The truth is that "love" is spelled t-i-m-e—just ask any parent. It's the same way with our heavenly parent. God wants to spend time with us; the question is, do we give our Sunday to God, or is Sunday the day we merely fit him in?

Don't feel guilty about really resting on Sunday. Truly resting one day a week is not only a form of prayer; it's a commandment. That doesn't mean that on Sunday you ignore other things that need to get done (like homework); it means you get it done prior to Sunday (yes, even on Friday or Saturday—perish the thought!). God loves you, but he doesn't love laziness. He loves our attention, not because he needs it, but because we do.

Salvation Given

And on the seventh day God finished the work that he had done, and he rested on the seventh day from all the work that he had

done. So God blessed the seventh day and hallowed it...
—GENESIS 2:2–3

So if you want to be like God, rest this Sunday. Who knew that a nap could make you holier?

Iron sharpens iron,

    and one man sharpens another.

—PROVERBS 27:17

Have you ever ridden a teeter-totter?

Solution Offered

When my best friend, Ronnie, moved away when I was six, I had no one to ride the teeter-totter (seesaw) with. Yep, that was me: the pitiful kid sitting on one side, the other side up in the air. C'mon, picture it. (As sad as it is, it has to make you laugh.)

The teeter-totter depends on one thing: a partner.

And just as important as that partner is for a successful teeter-totter experience, so a partner is equally important for our daily faith walk.

I'm not saying that our faith depends on another person but that the small successes of our faith journey, on a daily basis, can at times be dependent on our ability and willingness to call on another, to share with another, to have someone hold us accountable.

Last night I got a phone call from a really good friend. He was faced with a tough situation, a temptation. In his time of trial he called me.

That's accountability: sharing your walk, admitting weakness, looking for help, and allowing someone to hold you to a higher standard, the standard that God has set for you.

I love this verse. It is one of my favorites in all of Scripture. It's more than a wise saying; it is a universal truth, a challenge, and a call to action. Just as you'd sharpen your sword by the iron of another, so you can sharpen your spirituality by another's.

The holier I am, the holier those around me can become by leaning on me when times are tough. And the reverse is true: I can become stronger and holier through the example of others when times in my life become more difficult.

Know and trust this: Life is not meant to be a solo act. The teeter-totter of life is gonna have its ups and downs. Find yourself a strong partner, and enjoy the ride.

Salvation Given

Iron sharpens iron,
and one man sharpens another.
—Proverbs 27:17

Dare to share your walk.

Be on your guard toward your friends.

A faithful friend is a sturdy shelter:

  he that has found one has found a treasure.

There is nothing so precious as a faithful friend.

—SIRACH 6:13–15

Friendship is a tricky thing. There are, for most people, many different levels of friendship. Who considers you a friend? On a scale of one to ten (ten being the best), what kind of a friend are you? How do your friends rank?

Solution Offered

When I got involved in Life Teen (my youth group) during high school, I basically had my "regular" friends and my "church" friends. It wasn't that the "church" friends were bad people, just that they weren't as popular or cool as some of my _other_ friends, whom I hung out with more often.

After a while I began to realize that the people whom I respected most, trusted most, and could really talk to had one thing in common: They were the ones sitting next to me at Mass or on a retreat. My two worlds were colliding.

Ever felt that way? This verse is really simple yet so profound. "Be on guard with your friends," it says. Why? You and I both know why. We've all had friends who brought us down at times, even if we didn't want to admit it.

When you look back years from now, you might find (as I do) two kinds of friends that you remember: the kind who helped you grow and the kind who stunted your growth. I'm not saying that all your friends have to be "church" friends; just that when you have *God* in common, other stuff comes naturally, goes deeper. Read the verse again. Make sense?

Pick out one or two people who've been faithful friends to you, and text them (or better yet, call them)—and thank them. Help someone grow today.

Salvation Given

Be on your guard toward your friends.
A faithful friend is a sturdy shelter:
   he that has found one has found a treasure.
There is nothing so precious as a faithful friend.
—SIRACH 6:13–15

You've got a friend in Jesus (and in me).

Um, I'm asking for a friend...

> He said to them, "Come away to a deserted place all by your-
> selves and rest a while." For many were coming and going, and
> they had no leisure even to eat.
> —MARK 6:31

Are you friends with any cranky people? Do you ever get cranky? I sure
do.

Solution Offered

Okay, I admit it—sometimes, very rarely (and by rarely, I mean often),
I can get cranky.

It's funny, isn't it, how when someone accuses us of being in a bad
mood, our immediate response (yours and mine) is usually, "No, I'm
not!" We're so quick to deny it, especially when it's true. Sometimes we
don't see it. Other times, we see it but don't want to admit it.

(Side note here to those readers who never get cranky—pray for
those of us that do, OK?)

What are the two leading causes of crankiness in my life? That's easy:

Lack of food

Lack of sleep

When I'm overly hungry, the crank starts to set in, and when I haven't
gotten enough sleep, it's the same story—the crank rears its ugly head.

This verse from St. Mark's Gospel, upon first glance, might just be
a narrative piece explaining what Jesus said and what the apostles did.
I believe, however, that it teaches us far more. This isn't just a retelling
of what they were supposed to do but, more to the point, who God
wanted them to be. Notice that it doesn't even say that the apostles

were cranky. Picture the scene, though. Really think about it. The apostles had been ministering all day long, and they were so busy that they hadn't eaten or slept. They had spent hours upon hours taking care of others with no thought of themselves or their own physical needs. I've had days like that, and I ended up very tired and quite cranky.

Notice how Jesus taught them to deal with their fatigue and hunger before it became an issue. Jesus understood the importance of taking care of ourselves physically, not only spiritually. Jesus also demonstrated the need to feed ourselves (not just spiritually, but physically) before we could feed others.

Maybe, just maybe, that's one of the reasons that in God's great wisdom, he commands (not requests) that we "keep holy the Sabbath." God, as our Creator, knows what we truly need to be healthy. Which maybe, just maybe, is why the Eucharist is such an indispensable and vital part of every Mass. It's true in this case (and in all cases) that our "Father knows best."

He wants us to rest. He wants to feed us at his table. Every Mass, he is basically saving us from ourselves—weekly, even daily—when we let him. He's a great dad, making sure that his kids get their rest and eat right.

I'm just glad that Christ, in his divine humanity and human divinity, was around to set us straight with some solid Christian advice: "Come... rest...eat."

Salvation Given

He said to them, "Come away to a deserted place all by yourselves and rest a while." For many were coming and going, and they had no leisure even to eat.

—MARK 6:31

Maybe that's why I love that nap after the Thanksgiving meal. Oh, by the way, the Greek word eucharist means "thanksgiving"—see how intimately connected eating, prayer, and sleeping are in the mind of God?

Take your foot off the gas.

Therefore do not be anxious about tomorrow, for tomorrow will
be anxious for itself. Let the day's own trouble be sufficient for
the day.

—MATTHEW 6:34

Do you have a busy life? Do you have a full schedule? Do you sometimes feel that you just don't have enough hours in the day? Feeling a
little stressed or overextended?

Solution Offered

In this verse, Jesus offers simple truth to an age-old problem. Now,
to understand this verse, we have to put it into context. These words
from our Lord come straight out of his famous Sermon on the Mount.
He's already spoken to the crowds about the Beatitudes, given them
the Lord's Prayer, and reminded them of God's love. Then, all of the
sudden, Jesus drops this truth bomb—one that is as timeless as it is
practical.

Put simply, Jesus tells us not to stress and not to overextend ourselves.

Pause and reflect on this reality for a second. The God of the universe
is talking to them (and us) about the worthlessness of stress and dangers
of overwork. Why, you may ask? Because these were spiritual traps
and real problems for people even two thousand years ago! The apostles even took on too much. They had been working hard (as we read
about in the previous entry. Busyness doesn't just breed crankiness (as
we saw), but it hands stress the keys to our house and invites him in to
stay awhile.

Jesus knew well that stress doesn't bring anything but greater stress and that doing more than God asks on a given day is a recipe for disaster. Purgatory is filled with people who did more than God asked. If God wants something done, he will provide a way for it to get done. He didn't want his disciples (then or now) thinking it was all about them. What a great reminder for us to rely more on God and to trust in his love for us and his greater plan (especially for those of us control freaks who tend to take on too much in the name of God and ministry).

How about you? Do you get so busy at work, or at school, or with sports or other activities that you push yourself too hard? Is that what Jesus is calling us to do? Or is he calling you to freedom in this verse? I hear constantly from people who are overworked or too busy, people who don't take enough time to rest or sleep. "There's just too much to do!" I hear (and say).

Jesus is reminding us that there will always be need. He reminds us that it isn't all dependent on us and that we cannot put our energy into fruitless things (like stress) or worry over potential problems (tomorrow) that may never occur. This passage is not only an invitation to exhale and trust God, but also a reminder to be present to today!

Jesus is giving you, as his follower, permission to slow down. Take it easy today, or this weekend, if you can. Take a retreat, or reschedule things and sleep in. Sit and watch one of your favorite movies. Turn off your phone. Read a book. Get out and exercise. Indulge in your favorite snack. Sit back and enjoy the world God created.

Relax, and don't worry, just for one day. You will be a better Catholic Christian for it.

Thank God the whole time you're doing it, and don't feel guilty. Rest up this weekend, because God has plans to use you next week. How do I know? Because God has plans to use you every week.

Don't get me wrong: Jesus worked hard. But in his wisdom, he knew when to laugh, to sleep, and to rest…and he knew never to stress.

Salvation Given

Therefore do not be anxious about tomorrow, for tomorrow will be anxious for itself. Let the day's own trouble be sufficient for the day.
—MATTHEW 6:34

Smell the roses. God created them.

> The Spirit helps us in our weakness; for we do not know how to pray as we ought, but the Spirit himself intercedes for us with sighs too deep for words.
>
> —ROMANS 8:26

Do you ever get frustrated when you try to pray because things just don't come out of your mouth right? When you hear somebody else pray, do you ever say, "I wish I could pray like that," or, "I don't know how to say those things. I sound stupid when I pray"? Sometimes it can be intimidating to pray out loud, especially in front of a group of people, if you're not used to it.

Solution Offered

In this verse, St. Paul is telling the Romans that it doesn't matter what words they use when they pray, because if they (like us) are doing it right (with our hearts, that is), then the Holy Spirit surrounds our prayer with its own language. Paul tells us that the Holy Spirit intercedes for us and speaks in sighs that are too deep for words.

God doesn't care what wording or phrasing you use when you're talking to him. God knows our hearts. God knows you better than you know yourself.

Tonight when you pray, try something different. Don't be too concerned with the words—he knows all. Instead, why don't you do less talking and more listening?

Sometimes we just need to shut up when we pray. Spend some time in silence tonight with the Lord, and let him really speak to you. Listen with your heart for more than a voice. If you don't hear anything at first, it's OK; just stay silent. Let God do the talking, and let him have the last word.

Salvation Given

> The Spirit helps us in our weakness; for we do not know how to pray as we ought, but the Spirit himself intercedes for us with sighs too deep for words.
> —ROMANS 8:26

God gave us each two ears and one mouth so we'd listen twice as much as we talk!

FINDING
GOD
IN THE
EVERYDAY

He's everywhere...
just take
a look

Is the Snooze Button a Gift from God or a Trap from the Devil?

You snooze, you lose.

You know what time it is, how it is now the moment for you to wake from sleep. For salvation is nearer to us now than when we became believers.
—ROMANS 13:11, NRSV

Have you ever overslept? Have you ever gotten into trouble because of the snooze button?

Solution Offered

Ah, the snooze button! It's either your best friend or your personal demon. To be honest, speaking for myself, if a dog is man's best friend, I'd have to vote the snooze button number two.

You know how it goes:

Maybe you stayed up late getting work done...

Maybe you couldn't turn off that stupid movie at 2:00 A.M....

Maybe you were texting or online half the night...

Whatever the reason, you couldn't pull yourself out of bed the next morning. The sun crept through your window like an unwanted intruder, signaling to you that it was time to join the living. You fought it. With your eyes still closed and your hand searching around the nightstand for that annoying contraption responsible for that awful noise, you finally (with a groggy voice) began to awaken. Muttering something that sounds like "ten more minutes," you then retreated back under the covers after slapping the top of the clock or the face of your phone. You return to your slumber for six hundred more seconds of bliss.

One problem, though.

Sooner or later you have to get up, you have to join the living. You know it. I know it. Your boss/teacher/parent/anyone else waiting for you knows it. You can't escape it forever.

I constantly try to hit the snooze button in my spiritual life. It's more comfortable to avoid responsibility. It's always more comfortable to do what I want and say, "Give me some more time, God; then I'll be there for you."

Too many of us have our faith life on snooze. But we can't go through life with our eyes closed. We can't put life off any longer. We can't hide in the dark when the Son is waiting for us. St. Paul reminds us that there is an urgency to our lives, and with that urgency comes an expectation. Now is the acceptable time of salvation—now is the acceptable time to answer God's call. In other words, we should not put off until tomorrow what God calls us to today. As St. Paul reminds the Christians in Rome in this passage, now is the hour to awaken!

That's why we have seasons like Advent and Lent, to kick the mattress when we have been hitting the spiritual snooze button. The Church is our mother, and she loves us too much to let us lazily sleep our lives away when there is service to be done and souls to be reached in Christ's name. It's the Church giving us God's wake-up call, to get us going so we're all awake for whatever mission the Lord puts before us today.

Salvation Given

> You know what time it is, how it is now the moment for you to wake from sleep. For salvation is nearer to us now than when we became believers.
> —Romans 13:11, NRSV

The fact that you are reading this means you woke up today. The fact that you woke up today means that God isn't done with you yet. He has a mission for you—a mission only you can fulfill. Lose the snooze and get to it.

But as for me, I am filled with power,
  with the Spirit of the Lord,
  and with justice and might.
—Micah 3:8

Do you go through a lot of batteries?

Solution Offered

When did I become so lazy?

Last week the batteries in my TV remote died. I don't mind saying it was devastating.

What was I supposed to do? Walk the eight feet to the television and turn the channels by hand? How absurd! I stubbornly moved the batteries around, slapped the remote control a couple times, pressed the buttons harder (like that was gonna help)—but nothing worked.

So I pulled one battery out. It had one of those little power measuring meters on it, so I touched the two dots and squeezed, hoping to see the reassuring message "Good" pop up in the window. Nothing—there was no energy left in that battery.

It got me thinking. If God put his hand around me and touched my head and heart, what word would come up? Would it read "Good"? My spiritual battery gets low on power, too, and sometimes may even seem dead. Of course, no matter how low it is, because of my baptism it can never die. It just needs to be recharged every so often.

The more I allow God into my life, the stronger my battery becomes, going from "good" to "very good" to "great" to "unstoppable." The catch is, I have to seek the outlet (God) and plug in (let God form me).

If you're at one of those low points right now, where you're not really excited about the faith or are having a hard time, then it's time to plug in and recharge the batteries.

If you're running strong right now, then look around, find someone who needs a jump start, and help them to tap in.

When the batteries in my remote died, I felt helpless, and I couldn't function. But when my spiritual battery is low, I realize how helpless I truly am. Coincidence?

Salvation Given

But as for me, I am filled with power,
    with the Spirit of the Lord,
    and with justice and might.
—MICAH 3:8

Ever notice how most power outlets have three separate holes, but they're all one? Feels like the Holy Trinity is reminding me to plug in.

When I look at your heavens, the work of your fingers,
the moon and the stars that you have established;
what are human beings that you are mindful of them,
mortals that you care for them?
Yet you have…
given them dominion over the works of your hands.
—PSALMS 8:3–6, NRSV

When's the last time you colored?

Solution Offered

I was a great colorer. (And to all of you saying, "That's not a word"—
it is now).

I'm serious. I was a genius with a crayon. The use of multiple colors,
shading, always staying inside the lines…at the risk of being prideful, I
was truly great, well ahead of my years. People would come from miles
away just to view my work. Each new piece of art graced and adorned
the front of the family refrigerator for days.

Then I turned seventeen, and Mom said, "You're getting too old to
color, Mark. Go get a job."

That was the day the coloring ceased, the day my crayons died. Alas,
I would never use those sixty-four Crayolas again.

Okay, so I may have exaggerated pretty much every single detail
in that story. The truth is that I had no technique. I always colored
outside the lines, no matter how hard I tried, and I only had about fifty
crayons…I may have fed the family dog the rest. Hey, don't judge me
(see Matthew 7:1).

Not too long ago, I was coloring with my youngest daughter, and I asked her, "Why did you use this color here, and this color over here?" She replied, "Because that's just how it looks in my head. Isn't it pretty?"

Looking at her picture, the pink frog didn't make any sense to me, nor did the blue cow. She hadn't colored inside the lines; she hadn't even colored the whole picture. People were missing noses, and their eyes were disproportionate to the rest of their faces. Van Gogh was rolling over in his grave. Michelangelo was covering his eyes. Picasso she was not...she was even better! Every line, color, and stroke was an exterior expression of her interior heart. Everything in that picture, though imperfect, told me something about its beautiful young artist.

Sure, I could have found a thousand problems with it from my adult and more critical point of view, but why? Love created the picture, and love was all I could see on that page or in her eyes. To her, the picture was a work of art; it was beautiful, and she wanted me to have it. She created a work of art out of her love for me, and it was scribbled not only on the sheet in front of me, but all over her face, too.

Sometimes when I look at the world, I get too caught up in asking, "What's wrong with this picture?" I see everything that is off, rather than all that is beautiful within it. I might wonder why God made this person this way, or why he didn't stay inside the lines over here. I forget that when everything was created, it really was a work of art...everything was beautiful, and God wanted us to have it because he loves us. It's not God's fault that sin entered the picture. God makes all things beautiful, and God can even make a work of art out of our crooked (and sinful) lines if we let him.

That's what today's Scripture reminds me of—that God, the Creator, uses his creation to point us back to him. The heavens and the moon and the stars—all of creation—echoes the beauty of the one who created them. The heavens are an arrow to heaven, if we have the eyes to see it. God uses everything within creation, including you and me, to lead souls back to him. Do you consider yourself a work of art in God's eyes? You are. Even when you've made mistakes. Even though you're not perfect, God the Father sees the beauty and love within you. He doesn't criticize you, he doesn't point out your flaws…he just sits back and rejoices over his child.

Today, look at the sky, the plains, the mountains, the stars—perhaps stop and watch the sunset. Thank God for coloring so beautifully and for finding such beauty in us even when we color imperfectly.

Salvation Given

When I look at your heavens, the work of your fingers,
   the moon and the stars that you have established;
what are human beings that you are mindful of them,
   mortals that you care for them?
Yet you have…
   given them dominion over the works of your hands.
—Psalms 8:3–6, NRSV

And never, ever stop coloring.

Bring forth the people who are blind, yet have eyes,
   who are deaf, yet have ears!
—Isaiah 43:8

Do you ever lose the signal on your cell phone while you're talking? It's pretty annoying, huh?

Solution Offered

Some people call them dead zones. They are the areas where you lose your cell phone signal in the middle of a conversation. Talk about frustrating.

When it happens, I usually end up spending the next five or so minutes moving my head and phone (an inch at a time) in weird angles to try to regain the signal. It's usually a case of the other person still being able to hear me, even though I can't hear him or her. The conversation is basically "Hello...Can you hear me?" and "Are you there?"

What's even worse is when I know that I'm about to drive through a dead zone, and rather than pull my car over, I just drive through it anyway and stubbornly attempt to keep talking (frustrating myself and the person I'm speaking with).

I have these dead zones in my spiritual life, too.

I can be doing great in my prayer life and in my faith journey, but then I actively do or say things that weaken my relationship with God. Deciding to go through a dead zone disrupts my communication with our Lord and the overall strength of my (spiritual) signal. I know he can still hear me, but I can no longer hear him, deafened as I am by my wants and needs.

I look at the little bar indicators on my cell phone that tell how strong my signal is and think about how I kind of have one of those indicators imprinted on my soul, too.

I know when I'm choosing to enter a dead zone; I know when I can't hear his voice as clearly as I did before. The question is, "What do I do about it? And when?"

The bad news is that in my pride, I usually wait a lot longer than I should to do anything (dumb move).

The beauty of it is that God never gives up or hangs up. He waits, with patience, until I can move out of that dead zone and get to a better location in my life.

So next time you're on a cell phone with someone and one of you hits a dead zone, stop, take a second, and say a prayer of thanks to God for never hanging up on us.

Salvation Given

Bring forth the people who are blind, yet have eyes,
who are deaf, yet have ears!
—ISAIAH 43:8

Speaking for God, like any parent, I think he's just really glad when we take the time to call.

His disciples had gone to the city to buy food.

—JOHN 4:8

Can you picture Jesus in a grocery store?

Today's verse is one of those tiny little verses that we often overlook in the midst of a larger story. It's often in the smallest and simplest ways, however, that God reveals his greatest truths—look no further than the manger.

This verse tells us that Jesus's disciples went into town to buy some food. Think about it, they had to go grocery shopping. Now, although it doesn't say that Christ went with them, I am still trying to picture grocery shopping with Jesus. How insanely cool would that be?

I bet he'd never pick the cart with the wobbling wheel. He'd select all the freshest fruit. What kind of cereal would he like? What would his favorite brand of peanut butter be? I bet he'd always pick the quickest checkout line, too.

The reason I bring this verse up is very simple: Sometimes when we picture Christ's divinity, we lose sight of his humanity. Yes, Jesus was completely God, 100 percent—no question about it, but Jesus was also completely man, 100 percent human in all things but sin (Hebrews 4:15).

Too often we forget that Christ (or any biblical figure, for that matter) was human. Jesus got tired. He got hungry. He experienced stress. He got sunburns and stomachaches and sore throats. He experienced hardship, sadness, temptation, and suffering. Jesus experienced all of those things and more; Jesus was all God and all human. Jesus would have had chores to do growing up. Jesus had to find food to eat and take time to cook and make time to bathe and find time to sleep. He had physical needs like we all do.

Sometimes when I read the Scriptures, I have a tendency to think of Old and New Testament characters as fictional characters, rather than as actual people who lived very real and very difficult lives. Today, no matter what happens or what emotions flow through you, remember that Jesus the God-man knows what you're going through. Offer up the headache, the stomachache, the stress, the hunger, the exhaustion, and the temptation to the one who knows what you are going through.

Salvation Given

His disciples had gone to the city to buy food.
—JOHN 4:8

Now, picture Jesus doing the dishes—that's biblical, too. If you don't believe me, check out 2 Kings 21:13.

[So] that through these you may escape from the corruption that is in the world because of evil passion…make every effort to supplement your faith with virtue, and virtue with knowledge, and knowledge with self-control, and self-control with steadfastness.

—2 Peter 1:4–6, JB

Ever feel like your faith life is boring or has lost its flavor? Ever wonder why?

Solution Offered

I love gum. I mean it, I really do. As a kid, I always had gum in my mouth (and sometimes in my hair, but that's another story).

If someone asked you to describe what gum is like, what would you say? How would you describe it? It's hard to find the words, huh?

You might say, "It's something with flavor that you chew on." They might ask back, "Why do you chew it?" "Well, the whole point of gum is to chew it." "OK, but why?" "Well, that's the whole point of gum… to be chewed."

Gum is kind of like faith.

When gum (faith) loses its flavor (excitement), we just throw it out, because it's stale (boring), or we're tired of chewing (putting in effort). The difference is that faith is like a gum which the more we chew (put in effort), the more flavor (strength) we experience—and we'll never throw it out. It just takes constant effort.

Maybe you can't explain what your faith is like, only that you know it's there and that it's always good to have a little with you for when you really need it—just like gum.

Now, read this verse again. What is St. Peter telling us to do?

Look around and see the evil desires in people and in the world that take our attention away from God.

Put effort into our faith.

Supplement (grow and mature) in our faith.

This doesn't apply just to teens or young adults; this is a call to everyone, regardless of age, experience, or openness. We're all on a journey of faith: Some are walking, some running, some standing still, but we're all on a path.

So how do we survive the evils of the world? Tell 'em again, St. Peter: effort.

That's right, effort. We need to mature in our faith by growing in virtue (leading a moral life), in knowledge (reading and studying the Scriptures), in self-control (controlling our speech, emotions, and, yes, sexuality), and in steadfastness (never quitting or giving up on God, no matter how hard it gets). That's how we grow.

Salvation Given

> [So] that through these you may escape from the corruption that is in the world because of evil passion …make every effort to supplement your faith with virtue, and virtue with knowledge, and knowledge with self-control, and self-control with steadfastness.
> —2 PETER 1:4–6

If your faith has lost its flavor, put in a new piece (reconciliation) and start chewing.

Your word is a lamp to my feet,
a light on my path.
—Psalm 119:105, JB

Have you ever had to find your way around in the dark?

It can be tough, especially if you aren't exactly sure where you are going.

Solution Offered

So I woke up in the middle of the night this week, half-asleep and thirsty, and went to the kitchen to get some water. I wanted to go right back to sleep, so I was keeping my eyes closed as much as I could (ever do that?) and was sort of feeling my way to the kitchen. As I walked, I stubbed my toe on the wall. *Ouch!* (And that is what I said.)

It hurt really bad, but I didn't know how badly I had wounded it until I opened the refrigerator door. The light spilled out and exposed a very, very sore foot, swelling up and turning a lovely shade of purple.

When I saw how bad the injury was, I quickly grabbed some ice and hobbled over to the couch. There I sat, awake and in pain and annoyed that I had left my comfortable, warm, and safe bed to venture into the darkness, too stubborn to turn on a light. Good call, BG.

After hobbling into church for Mass the next day, I had to kind of laugh when we sang, "Thy word is a lamp unto my feet." Too bad I hadn't been carrying a Bible into the kitchen, huh?

It is an interesting comparison, though. The Word of God is a light in the darkness—the darkness of a world that can be pretty selfish and pretty sick at times.

As disciples of Christ, we are called to go out into the world and preach the Good News of Christ through not only words but also actions. The world can be a dark place, which is why the Word of Christ is so important. When we hold the Word deep within our hearts and apply the truth of the Bible to our everyday lives, we not only have our light in the darkness, we are a light in the darkness. The better we learn and hold fast to Scripture, the less we will stub our toes on stupid sins. We will see clearly enough to avoid the walls and to know when to turn corners.

Spend a few minutes in the Bible this weekend, and see what God is telling you. It's dangerous in the dark, but we have nothing to fear when we stand in the light, his light.

Salvation Given

Your word is a lamp to my feet,
    a light on my path.
—PSALM 119:105, JB

In my house, the flashlight is just a place to keep dead batteries.

> For ever, O Lord, your word
> is firmly fixed in the heavens.
> —PSALM 119:89

A lot of people think that the Bible is an out-of-date book that has no application in the so-called real world. But I'll bet you or your parents have quoted Scripture at times and not even known it.

Solution Offered

Let me show you what I mean. There are a lot of common phrases we use today that have their roots in God's book, the Bible. How many of these have you heard?

The blind leading the blind (see Matthew 15:14)

Turn the other cheek (see Matthew 5:39)

By the skin of your teeth (see Job 19:20)

Holier than thou (see Isaiah 65:5)

A leopard can't change his spots (see Jeremiah 13:23)

The powers that be (see Romans 13:1, KJV)

Keep on the straight and narrow (see Matthew 7:14)

Am I my brother's keeper? (see Genesis 4:9)

Keep the faith (see 2 Timothy 4:7)

The Good Samaritan (see Luke 10:30–37)

Eat, drink, and be merry (see Ecclesiastes 8:15)

Armageddon (see Revelation 16:16)

A wolf in sheep's clothing (see Matthew 7:15)

The writing on the wall (see Daniel 5)

The apple of one's eye (see Deuteronomy 32:10)

A drop in the bucket (see Isaiah 40:15)

An eye for an eye (see Exodus 21:22–24)

Nothing new under the sun (see Ecclesiastes 1:9)

A scapegoat (see Leviticus 16:8–10)

Woe is me! (see Isaiah 6:5)

Even a lot of non-Catholic Christians do not read their Bible every day. But the Bible is the bestselling book in history, published in more languages than any other, surviving countless people and wars that have tried to destroy it.

Unfortunately, many times people are right when they accuse Catholics of not knowing their Bibles. The good news, however, is that it doesn't have to be that way.

Reading this book of Scripture meditations is a fine first step, but you can't stop here. Crack open the Book. Then go on to the *Catechism of the Catholic Church* and other books that help you understand the Bible. Ask priests for guidance; ask youth ministers and anyone in your church who may know a lot about Scripture.

I never want to be considered a lazy Catholic, and I don't think that you do either. I pledge to all of you, especially to you teens, to open my Bible every day and read the Word of God, even if it's only for a couple of minutes. Who's with me?

Salvation Given

For ever, O Lord, your word
   is firmly fixed in the heavens.
—Psalm 119:89

Here I am, God. I beg you to set me on fire for your Word.

He covers his hands with the lightning,
and commands it to strike the mark.
—JOB 36:32

Does God bowl? You might not know this, but bowling is Catholic.

Solution Offered

During thunderstorms as a kid, my grandfather said that the cracks of thunder were caused by God bowling up in heaven. It seemed to make perfect sense at the time. To this day, whenever I go bowling or see a thunderstorm, I remember my grandpa's words.

Honestly, I love bowling; it's the only sport where wearing rented shoes is normal, and athletes eating fattening, greasy food while playing is not only allowed but encouraged. In bowling, even the greatest athletes can lose to the least coordinated, least athletic souls on the planet. Those gutters are a great social equalizer—alleys of grace where nerds with a comprehension of physics can finally emerge victorious over more physically gifted souls on a wax-laned field of battle.

What you also may not know is that many credit the invention of bowling to a Catholic saint—St. Boniface to be exact.

While St. Boniface was trying to convert the German hordes to Christianity around A.D. 300, he began evangelizing them by adopting some of their customs. At the time many of the Germans walked around with sticks called *kegels* and, as a game, they would throw them at smaller sticks called *heides*.

Just as our Lord Jesus would use the things around him—be it a fig tree, a vine, a flower, or a bird—to teach people about the love of God, Boniface sought to do the same. The great saint taught the pagan hordes about the Christian truth of good versus evil through this sport with the *kegels* and *heides*. He changed the significance of the game by making the smaller sticks represent demons. When a person successfully rolled their stick, knocking down the others, Boniface told them that it showed "purity of Spirit." Our modern game of bowling is a direct adaptation of the game that St. Boniface perfected. History is silent as to whether or not St. Boniface wore a bowling shirt, but I like to think of him in one.

Maybe the idea of God in heaven bowling during thunderstorms isn't that far-fetched after all. Maybe, just maybe, St. Boniface is up there playing, too. I'll bet St. Anthony is even around…the Lord knows how many times I have prayed and asked him to help me find a bowling ball that fit my fingers.

While this verse from Job obviously isn't actually about bowling, it's one of those biblical verses that reminds me of something in my everyday life. Scripture is great that way. God can draw us back to him in both direct and indirect ways through his Word, if we have the eyes to see and the ears to hear. Each time I drive by the bowling alley now, I think of these words from Job, and it turns my thoughts to God.

I think it's OK with God if I take this verse a little out of context. He's just excited that something like bowling can get me thinking about him. Next time you bowl, I hope you will, too.

Salvation Given

He covers his hands with the lightning,
  and commands it to strike the mark.
—Job 36:32

Someone once said that analogies like this are stupid and that God is too busy to play games or have fun. My response? Oh, spare me.

Listen to me;
be silent, and I will teach you wisdom.
—JOB 33:33

Have you ever gotten lost when driving the car? Have you ever been given poor directions or gotten turned around when trying to find someplace for the first time? Me, too.

Solution Offered

It never fails. Now, I consider myself pretty good with directions, and I don't get lost very often. But whenever I'm in a hurry or don't listen closely enough to directions, I end up driving in circles.

And you know what I do when I'm driving and lost? I turn the radio down.

That's right. When I'm lost, I always seem to turn down the radio. Why do I do that? How and why is the radio connected to my ability to navigate? I don't just do it to hear the GPS, either; I think I do it to hear myself think. It's as if I can concentrate better without the additional noise.

Look at this verse; this is God speaking to you, just as directly as he did to Job so many years ago. We all get turned around sometimes. We get going in one direction (which is probably the wrong direction), but the secret to getting where we need to be is turning down the radio, silencing all of the noise of the world around us and just being quiet.

If you're like me, you have a very busy life, filled with people who want or need your time and attention. It can all get pretty noisy. Also, if you're like me, you probably don't take as much silent time as you could—time with no phone, television, or music around you.

Do yourself a favor this week. Turn off your music when you're in the car, and just allow God to speak to you in the silence. When you're at home tonight, go to bed earlier than normal, before you're falling asleep. And instead of talking to God, listen to him.

And sometime this week, don't tell anybody, but get to a church on your own when it's empty. Take fifteen or twenty minutes when no one's around. Sit in silence in the house of God. Let him do the talking.

Whether or not you're lost right now, it never hurts to turn that radio down.

Salvation Given

Listen to me;
   be silent, and I will teach you wisdom.
—JOB 33:33

God can be so loud in the silence. Give him a chance.

I will instruct you and teach you
  the way you should go;
I will counsel you with my eye upon you.
—PSALM 32:8

Ever feel like God is slowing you down? Do you ever get impatient with God and his plan for you? Ever tell God that if he'd just tell you what to do you'd do it?

Solution Offered

I was stuck in traffic the other morning and really annoyed. I was annoyed because I was in a hurry and had a lot of work to do: God's work.

I couldn't be slowed down for anything. I mean, "For the love of… well, him!" This was his *work*!

When I finally got out of traffic and made it into the parking lot, I got really frustrated. Speed bumps.

I hate speed bumps. I mean, I hate them. They're so annoying, and they slow me down when I have things to do.

I exhaled and began to get angry. Then I saw a dog run across my path. At that moment I was thankful for the speed bump. Had it not been there, I may have hit that dog.

Just then, I had a realization. There are a lot of speed bumps in my spiritual life—a lot of little obstacles, little trials God sets before me to slow me down and force me to look around.

I don't know about you, but when I get going on something, I can get so focused on it that I don't fully realize what's happening around me. Sometimes I'm so focused on my life that I forget others and their